SOUNDS
FROM THE
CADDIE
YARD

BY
MIKE ECKHARD
THE GOLFMAN

ISBN: 1-57502-523-X
Library of Congress Catalog Card Number: 97-90659

Additional copies are available.
For your convenience, an order form
can be found at the back of this book.

Cover designed by Mike Eckhard, Jr.

Edited by Martie Eckhard Anderson

Printed in the USA by

MORRIS PUBLISHING
3212 East Highway 30 • Kearney, NE 68847 • 1-800-650-7888

To all the Rock and Muny Caddies

Writing about my caddie days is somewhat like the story of the 85 year old woman who called the police station and reported that she had been raped. The police sergeant said, "when did this happen, ma'am?" She replied, "June 17, 1929 at 11:30 p.m." And he answered, "we can't do anything about it now." She said, "I know it, but I like to talk about it." Though it's been over 50 years since I left the caddie ranks, I still like to talk about it. Hope you find it interesting.

This book is about my caddie days from the summer of 1928 to the fall of 1939. The country was in a depression all of these years and it made caddying quite competitive. The opportunity for a kid to earn 35 cents to $2.00 a day was considered big time. These were the days when the family bread winner's average weekly earnings were about $18.00. You were considered to have a real good job if you made $25.00 a week. However, this type of work usually required you to put in 60 to 80 hours a week.

Most caddies helped put food on the table by donating their earnings or at least part of their earnings to the family cause. All my caddie days, I gave my Mom 50% of my earnings and bought most of my clothes with the other half. I remember buying a white golf style cap each summer at a downtown dry goods store (Snyders).

The price was 19 cents plus a penny tax. In those days, I don't remember caps being made adjustable. My size was 6 7/8.

Golf course caddies are a dying breed. Motorized golf cars have done them in. An old saying goes, "if you've never had something, you'll never miss it." So true for golfers who took up the game long after caddies disappeared. There are some private country clubs which have not let their caddie program die. Some have had caddies available since the early 1900s. Other clubs which abandoned their caddie program are now heading a movement to "bring back the caddies". These country clubs recognize the vital role our youth play for a more enjoyable round of golf.

The area around the clubhouse without caddies sometimes gets as still as a morgue and as silent as a hospital zone. While those clubs who maintain caddies get an added quality of joy and service. The sounds from the caddie yard are a very worthwhile dimension of themselves: the shouts, the laughter that come from their fun games they play waiting for your tote. Caddies produce vibrations of excitement and enthusiasm that echo in the golf shop.

There is a crusade on to restore the caddie to the American scene. Resorts with bag carriers are reporting an increased demand. Applications for "Caddie Scholarships" are on the upswing. And the U.S. Golf Association has moved to start a "Caddie And Walking Committee". So I'm hoping for a caddie revival in the near future. I promise you golfers, a golf course with a good caddie program is the ticket for a much more enjoyable round of golf than what the motorized golf carts can provide.

WHAT YOU CAN EXPECT FROM A GOOD CADDIE

First of all, the player is out on the golf course to relax and enjoy the round. On the golf course, caddies make a valuable contribution of service. Carrying a bag full of golf sticks is but a small part of a caddie's job. Though he is a regular pack horse to carry up to 45 pounds of golf equipment over hilly and rugged terrain for 36 holes, if necessary; he does this chore without allowing the golf clubs to rattle or clack against each other.

He has a politician's desire to please everyone (money tips is his game). A caddie of the depression years of the 1930s had the street smarts of a good business man. He may comment to his player who just holed a 20 footer, "you looked like Bobby Jones on that one." Or when his player chips it to within two feet of the hole he might say, "just like Walter Hagen does it." Other than a few of these comments, he learns to keep his mouth shut and his eyes and ears wide open.

Since all the caddies at Rock Spring Country Club, where I spent ten full years in the caddie ranks, were boys, I'm writing this story in the masculine gender. Perhaps girls can do a good job caddying too. Nick Faldo takes one around the world to caddie for him. As I view her performance on TV with Nick's bag on her back, I'll have to say she does an excellent job.

If in the 1930s we had teenage girls in the caddie yard, I don't think it would've worked out. Why? You be the judge.

A good caddie makes himself plenty visible when needed and invisible when not.

His job is to replace divots and repair ball marks on the green and repair the tracks his player leaves in the sand bunkers.

He knows how to properly attend the flagstick. Seasoned golfers demand this. A caddie never steps closer than twelve inches from the hole whether he's holding the flagstick or retrieving his player's ball from the hole. He never steps in any player's line of putt and never lets his shadow appear in the line of the player putting. This requires the caddie to move around a bit and hold the flagstick with either hand.

When all players are close enough to see the hole, it's time to remove the flagstick. A good caddie removes it and goes to a spot some 20 to 50 feet away and watches the putting while holding the flagstick about three feet from the hole end and allows the flag end to rest on the green. This procedure keeps the wind from rustling the cloth flag making motion and noise. He must move around a bit should he be in the visual line of the player putting.

When all players have putted out, it comes time to replace the flagstick in the hole. A good caddie does this very carefully as not to damage the hole.

It's surprising how many holes are damaged today. Almost all rounds that I play, where the golf courses have no caddies, at least three or four holes have been damaged and sometimes all of them. Today's players step all over the hole, drag the ball out of the hole with their putter head and carelessly replace the flagstick. Some use the flagstick as a spear in replacing it. This act usually happens when a player misses a short putt and in his anger, sometimes takes a divot out of the green with the putter. Those guilty of these acts are not true golfers but FLOGGERS. FLOG is GOLF spelled backwards. It's not easy for the following group to grin and bear it. And it's not easy to accept someone abusing the golf course. There's one lesson all of us need to learn as we navigate through this world (and on the golf course) - we're going to be a victim of a lot of peoples' problems. We just need to make sure which one of us has the problem.

CARRYING THE GOLF BAG

Sounds simple enough, doesn't it? But there is a lot of things a caddie does once he's in charge of a bag full of golf sticks. While he carries it from one shot placement to another, as already mentioned, the clubs do not rattle or clack against each other. When they do, it's bothersome to most players. The caddie takes steps to reposition them in the golf bag.

A good caddie always knows where his player's ball is, and gets to it first. If a caddie wants to blow his tip, he trails his player a few yards and keeps talking. Upon a caddie's arrival at the ball, he first sets the golf bag in an upright position about six feet to the right of the ball (for a left handed player it's just the opposite) and about that same distance short. He hangs on to the top collar of the bag. Now the caddie is in the proper position as his player approaches. The player can get a good view of his line of play and select a club while there is not much chance of touching the ball with either one's feet. And should either caddie or player drop a club or the golf bag, neither will touch the golf ball. It's a stroke penalty should either accidentally move the golf ball. Some players get very uncomfortable when a caddie is standing too close to the ball.

Should the caddie be in the line of play of a player other than his, because of a shorter drive, he just stands aside and out of the danger zone with the bag in an upright position. His player gets the message that his caddie knows where his ball is. Meanwhile the caddie is taking a load off his shoulder and enjoying a short rest. You might be surprised to know a caddie spends more time with the bag off his shoulder than on it, conserving energy to go another round.

When golf balls are hit to the rough, woods, or out of bounds and can possibly be lost, a good caddie marks it's flight and landing zone by a post, tree, bridge, etc. and can usually arrive within a 25 feet circle of it making it as easy as possible to locate. Some golfers today miss an errant drive by as many as 100 yards. This requires help from other members of the foursome. This golfer is losing everybody's time. It's no wonder it takes six hours to complete 18 holes on a busy weekend. Slow play is the bitter topic echoing in the clubhouse.

We were so trained to keep an eye on the ball and mark it by something that we caddies seldom required the members to hunt for errant golf balls. Some scolded us when we couldn't locate their ball. One caddie was frantically hunting for his player's golf ball when the player arrived asking the caddie, "Didn't you mark it by something?" To which the caddie replied, "I marked it by a bird on the post, but the bird flew away."

CADDIES AND MEMBERS GOLF BALLS

Some caddies transferred golf balls from the golf bag ball pocket to their pants pocket. That's STEALING. And we got lectures from the pro on this subject quite often. Any caddie caught in the act got KICKED OFF (term for FIRED).

I did not steal golf balls. But I knocked several members' golf balls away. Those that I judged he'd never use again. And I knocked them away with his golf clubs. We were not allowed to swing member's golf clubs. I did. But they didn't see me.

When I did hit these balls in the woods, the devil's advocate that sits in the golfing brain guided me to this area the next day. We caddies called this "charity snitching". No sin attached as we were lightening the golf bag and making us more efficient caddies. Bill Cosby is right. Kids do have "brain damage".

A good caddie learns not to give advice unless he's asked. When a player asks, "what club do I need from here?" A good caddie will handle it this way by asking, "what club do you think it is?" If the player says, "I think it's a No. 7 iron shot" and the caddie knows it's a No. 5 shot, he says, "it's longer than that". If the player doesn't make a decision by selecting a club, hand him a

No. 6 iron and hope he hits it flush. Should he be short of the green, he'll know the caddie's choice was better than his.

We had one smart aleck caddie who was asked, "what club would you use from here?" To which he replied, "I'd hit a No. 8 iron but you better knock hell out of a No. 3 wood."

However, caddies do give some golf course advice, such as, "Sir, the distance from here to the flagstick is a little bit deceiving. Use one more club than you think it is." Or a caddie will mention things like, "This green is hard as a rock. Be careful your ball doesn't run over into the sand bunker behind the green." Or he may say something like this on a hole, "Sir, this is the slowest green on the golf course, rap your putt with a little bit more authority."

Now you have just read what kind of a performance you can expect out of a good caddie. So the round is over and it comes time to get paid. Please pay your caddie promptly. This too is a player's responsibility. I've waited for over an hour many times. Some guys took showers and changed clothes and had a drink or two before paying the caddie. Some caddie masters wouldn't listen to us calling to the locker room and telling the member to pay his caddie. We weren't allowed in the locker room.

I soon learned to tell the member, "I'd appreciate getting paid as soon as possible." And to some we tried some sympathy tactic. We would add, "I got to get to the grocery store before it closes to get a loaf of bread and a can of pork and beans."

Allow me to roll back the clock to the summer of 1926. It was then that my destitute family moved to a residence at the corner of Johnson and Wallace streets in middle town Alton, Illinois, just across the Mississippi River from St. Louis, Missouri. New to us, this home was four rooms and a path to a two-holer outhouse. No electricity then but it was coming in a year or two. We did have running water. Since I was born May 29, 1920, I am six years old. And soon learned, I was now living about the same distance from the then Number 7 green at Rock Spring Country Club as a good brassie shot for Bobby Jones.

Across the street lived another six year old, Bernard (Bud) Fahrig. The first day, we two rode around on our tricycles in circles too shy to speak though we were anxious to have each other as a friend. Little did we know this day that later that year we enrolled in the same first grade at the same Saint Mary's Catholic School, two miles away. We were the best of friends for many, many years. We walked back and forth to school together, caddied and played golf together and in later years, after both of us did a hitch in Uncle Sam's Army in World War II, we built a driving range in the area. It was called Mike & Bud's Golf Driving Range. It was located 3/4 of a mile north of North Alton on the Godfrey Road. It's subdivided today. Bud died in 1984. I lost a very dear friend.

Since my family lived less than 300 yards from the golf course and I was the youngest of nine children (an asset for mother leniency), it didn't take long to find the golf course. Finding the golf balls was thrilling. We waded in a shallow pond behind Number 7 green for errant golf balls that bounced out of bounds behind the green. Quickly we learned they could be sold for nickels and dimes which converts to penny candy and five cent soda pop. We kids got ambitious when we learned of profits selling golf balls. My mother would have killed me if she knew how far away from home I traveled as a seven year old. And too, going into the woods with briars and tall weeds in search of golf balls, I was exposing myself to snakes, hornets, spiders, chiggers, etc. At this tender age, I learned poison ivy had no effect on me. A great asset, when later, I became a caddie.

We kids in the neighborhood were all interested in golf, but there was only one kid in the neighborhood who owned a golf club. It was a hickory shafted mashie (today, called a No. 5 iron). He wasn't always available with it for our use. We did have some rinky-dink, nailed together golf clubs that more resembled hockey sticks. You've heard of golf ball hunting, but did you ever hear of anyone going golf club hunting? Well, we did. Here's what we youngsters would do. One parent had a workshop in his basement and we sneaked a hacksaw from it and went looking up in trees trying to locate a limb that was judged to be the right diameter and had a natural crook or branch that we could fashion into a homemade golf club. We'd climb the tree and saw off such a limb and finish it up on the ground. When we had made enough golf clubs so each kid had one, we returned the hack saw and no one ever knew we had borrowed it.

We had one kid who had a wooden walking cane that he used as a golf club. He was about four years older than me, say eleven or twelve. He could drive a golf ball about 100 yards with it. We played lots of golf in a neighborhood vacant lot where we laid out a six hole golf course. No hole on this course was longer than 40 yards. For the holes, we placed one pound coffee cans in holes dug out with our pocket knives. Early on, we didn't always have golf balls but played golf using jack balls, tennis balls, or cork balls. And sometimes we made our own balls by wrapping a rag around a small round rock (for weight) and binding it with old-fashioned electrician tape producing a ball a bit larger than a golf ball.

OTHER NEIGHBORHOOD GAMES

Kids in those days invented their own fun. There was no television and only a couple of radios in the whole neighborhood. All of the activity was outdoors. (Our home didn't have electricity or indoor plumbing at that time. I studied by lamplight.) We had all kinds of street games. Our street was an off street where cars passed at not more than three an hour. There were many horses and wagons using the city streets in the days of the late 1920s and early 1930s. The stock market crashed during this era and the country was in a depression all of my caddie days. One such driver of a horse pulling a wagon was an old codger who smoked a corncob pipe and at least once a week toured the neighborhood singing and shouting, "Rags, Rubber, Copper, and Old Iron". We kids collected these items and sold them to him.

Getting back to games kids played in the streets; some include "Tag", "Hide and Go Seek", "Kick the Can", and "Duck On A Rock". With a ball and bat we played "Peppers", "300", and occasionally chose up sides and played ball on a makeshift street diamond. A telephone pole was first base and home plate was a 30 inch diameter cast iron manhole cover. Our ball diamond wasn't exactly modern although the manhole cover was in the middle of the street and a street light hung from a telephone pole over it, lighting the diamond for games after dark.

The game of "Peppers" goes like this. We drew straws to see which kid got to bat. Then the rest of us (usually 6 to 8) lined up horizontally facing the batter with our feet about two feet apart. The feet of each kid in the line touched the feet of the kid on either side of him. The line of kids was about 15 feet from the batter. We'd toss the ball underhanded to the batter. He'd knock it back to us using a choked up bunting style stroke. If it got through your legs, it was an error and you went to the far right end of the line. If the ball went between two kids, both went to the end of the line. Since all the kids wanted to be the batter, the batter stayed at the plate until a pitch got by him. He then gave up the bat and went to the end of the line. The kid who was at the extreme left end of the line then became the batter and all moved one space left. The game proceeded in this fashion and usually everyone batted three or four times before the game broke up.

The game "300" was played as follows. There was one batter and one ball. However many other kids were fielders. The batter threw the ball in the air at his liking and swung at it. He hit some fly balls, some grounders, and some bouncers. The object was to get to bat and to do that, a fielder had to get 300 points. Then, the fielder and batter switched, all points canceled, and a new game started. Catching a fly ball counted 100. Catching a ball on the first bounce was 50. Fielding a grounder cleanly was worth 25. In your attempts to catch the ball, if you made an error, you were docked the amount of points that catch would have earned had you not fumbled it.

We played "Marbles", spun "Tops" and a whole lot of other made up games. We boys played with hoops and rolled automobile tires around. Girls played "Jacks", "Dolls", "Hopscotch" and "Jump Rope". We all had fun. I don't remember a fat kid in the neighborhood.

When I got to be 11 years old and we kids had a few golf clubs among us, we played golf in several pastures in the area. One golf course we fashioned was in the next block south of my home: Smith's pasture. We were able to lay out a three hole golf course. Number 1 was about 60 yards long, Number 2 was about 85 yards long, and Number 3 about 110 yards long. These holes were in somewhat of a triangle where Number 3 green was very close to Number 1 tee. We kept playing these holes over and over. At this time we practically abandoned the vacant lot six holer.

Most every evening in the summer months of 1931, '32, '33, and '34, the neighborhood kids congregated at Smith's pasture golf course after supper and we played until dark. At this time the cows were in the barn and no obstacle. However, their cow pies were hazards we don't have on golf courses today. A Baptist church at the corner of College Avenue and Johnson Street now stands on our then Number 3 green and it's parking lot covers the Number 1 hole.

Later on, we laid out a four hole golf course in St. Anthony's Infirmary pasture about 1/4 mile from my home. In those days, nuns milked the cows and we kids gave those gals fits. We would hit 150 yard golf shots trying to hit cows they were leading to the barn. These same nuns tended an orchard next to the pasture where we kids sampled the in-season fruits. Those nuns would've paddled our butts if only they could catch us. Please forgive me, Lord.

Rock Spring caddies had a makeshift golf course through part of Rock Spring Park. We also had a miniature golf course in the caddie yard. Since this little gem was real close to the golf shop, it got lots of play when we knew our names would be called for a tote.

My first caddie assignment was in the summer of 1928. At that time, I'm eight years old and very small for my age. I happened to tag along to the caddie yard one Saturday with a 12 year old neighborhood friend who had done some caddying. As it happened, they ran out of regular caddies that day and they used me. I earned 55 cents caddying for a lady who had a small, light bag. Being a green, talkative kid, she kept reminding me to keep quiet . This original experience both for earning real money and being a caddie will always live in my memories as perhaps the greatest day in my world of golf.

From then on, my mother didn't put the caddie yard off limits for me. I kept going there hoping they would again run out of "regular caddies". It didn't happen again in 1928. But it did happen twice in 1929. By this time I knew a bit more about caddying. Hanging around the caddie yard listening to older boys talk was big time to a nine year old. The older caddies gave me advice for me to improve as a caddie. And some advice about life I wasn't quite ready for. On Mondays, I caddied for free for caddies. They got to play golf every Monday from 7 a.m. until noon. They'd buy me a candy bar or a bottle of sodie (soda pop).

The caddie master wouldn't put my name on the LINE UP sheet as a nine year old. (I'll discuss LINE UP later.) He judged that I was too small or too green or both. Once I did get in the LINE UP at 7 am. Standing on my tip toes, the caddie master pointed to me and said, "Hey you, go home and eat some more biscuits." That was also a day of my world of golf I'll remember. One of the worst, as I went home crying. My Mom comforted me and said, "You'll grow up and get another chance." That advice at that time didn't sound too good to a nine year old ambitious kid who had gotten out of bed on his own at 5:30 am, hoofed it to the caddie yard, helped police the area around the clubhouse, and was rejected. As I think about this now, I realize it was probably the best lesson for me.

Kids get over bad days quickly. It just made me be more patient. And to get more in tune when I would get another chance to caddie. What the caddie master, who told me to 'go home and eat more biscuits' didn't know was, he was dealing with a kid who would become Rock Spring C.C. best caddie. "Best Caddie" was an award I won at the caddie annual banquet three years in a row: 1937, '38, and '39 when I was a veteran caddie. My caddie friends bestowed this honor to me on a secret ballot for this award. Help me. I'm choking to death patting myself on the back!

Hopefully, you readers are like myself in as much as when someone gets up in the pulpit to deliver a sermon, or when someone is giving a speech or writing an article or a book or just plain opening their mouth about any given subject, I want to know what kind of education and background they have from which they speak. So, surely my three years consecutive "Best Caddie" awards plus ten years in the caddie rank should qualify me for the previous pages where you're reading "what you can expect from a good caddie". I've done them all and a bit more.

While in the caddie ranks, I helped many caddies to perform better and gather bigger tips. I've gotten tips from players in our foursome other than my player. They seemed to be saying as they flipped me two bits, "I appreciate you being on the ball".

Let me tell you one more story. This story is true and happened in the late 1930s. I'm 17 or 18. At this time there are only two golf courses in the area which had a caddie program. Other than Rock Spring C.C., Alton Municipal Golf Course was it. There was a third golf course, Cloverleaf Golf Course but it had no caddie program. A golfer could bring his own caddie. There were days some of us Rock caddies hitch hiked to it (about 3 miles) on the Fosterburg Road. Incidentally, all three of these courses are operating today. Now there are nine golf courses in the immediate area.

On Wednesdays, a foursome played Cloverleaf who we knew would take caddies if we made ourselves available. We journeyed there several times - usually when we had high numbers on the LINE UP sheet and it was doubtful as to whether or not we'd get a tote at Rock.

Getting back to the story. Rock caddies and Muny caddies did many things together. We played golf together, played pool in upper Alton together, went to school together. We talked about the players we toted for and had them categorized. The big tippers, the tightwads, the grouches, etc. Well, one of the players who played regularly at Muny, had the moniker as being the biggest tightwad. These Muny caddies declared, "No caddie ever received a tip from him". This guy was W.R. Curtis, superintendent of the public school system. I learned later the teachers who he hired called him "Chisel Chin" as he hired them as cheap as possible and it was almost impossible to get a raise.

One day, the Kiwanis and Rotary Clubs had a tournament at Rock. I was assigned to the golf bag of Mr. Curtis. About 30 to 40 caddies were standing with their totes on Number 1 tee waiting for the tournament to begin. The caddies were giving me the haw haws and telling me "No tip today, Second Hand Man" (one of several nicknames caddies planted on me). The more they heckled me, the more determined I was to jar a tip from this guy. I reasoned, he being superintendent of schools, surely he knows it is customary to tip should he get the kind of performance to deserve one. And I reasoned, maybe he'd never had the kind of performance I was capable of giving him. All of the things you read a few pages back about what to expect from a good caddie, Mr. Curtis got this day. And he did shoot a very fine score.

Caddie fees at this time were 75 cents for 18 holes. I can almost count on my fingers and toes in the ten years in the caddie ranks, the times I received more than one dollar. One dollar was customary. That's a 25 cent tip. Pretty big in those days. However, many players gave a nickel tip, a dime tip or 90 cents was quite popular pay. We had some caddies who, if only tipped a nickel, would flip the nickel back to the player and say, "Here, you need this worse than I do."

Now it came time for Mr. Curtis to pay me. He gave me $1.25 - a 50 cent tip! I could not get one Muny caddie to believe me.

I have four sons (and two daughters) and I've told this story to all of them. One of my sons said, "Dad, I can understand why you were voted "best caddie". Ain't that nice?

To this story, I added, had I not gotten a tip from Mr. Curtis, I would have left the caddie yard knowing I gave him the best performance I knew how. Now when cutting grass, raking leaves, shoveling snow, carrying papers or any job, give a little bit more than is expected of you. It's the secret of success.

CADDIE FEES FORMAT THROUGH 1930

Prior to 1931, we caddies were paid by the hour: A-class 25 cents per hour, B-class 20 cents per hour. As a caddie was handed a golf bag, the caddie master also handed him a ticket with the time stamped on it. Our ticket started earning money from this moment on until it was again stamped at the time we returned the golf bag to the golf shop. As we were handed this ticket we were instructed to put it in our pocket or in the golf bag. At the finish of the round we handed it to the player. He signed it and checked a box describing our performance as: excellent, very good, good, fair, or poor. When our player had signed this ticket we were expected to go straight to the golf shop where the caddie master stamped the time the golf bag returned. He paid us at the above rates.

(Not realizing at the time, as an 8 year old and my first caddie assignment, the 55 cents I received was two hours, 45 minutes at B-class rate of 20 cents an hour. This was a 9 hole tote. You can easily see when the caddie fee format in 1931 changed to pay per 9 hole round @ 30 cents was a big cut in pay.)

When we were paid by the hour, caddies ran for bags belonging to the slowest players. Caddies were no dummies. The longer we were on the golf course, the more the ticket earned. We avoided these totes when paid per round. Or maybe they were dummies, as caddies wasted all the time they could getting from the last green to the golf shop. One trick the caddies pulled was to present their player with the ticket for signing as soon as possible in leaving Number 9 green (the last hole). Then lag back until the player got out of sight going to the locker room and then go to the BARN (This structure was once a barn to stable horses as the golf course was shaped with horse drawn equipment in the early 1900s and now was a maintenance shed.) and get a drink of water from a fountain there. Some caddies delayed getting to the golf shop by as much as 30 or 40 minutes. The BARN was located about 30 yards off Number 9 green and not too much out of the way of the route to the golf shop.

Caddies were unaware that they were being watched and this practice was stopped with the new caddie fee format. So you see, smart caddies out smarted themselves as the new fee format was a big, big cut in pay. Several A-class caddies took other more profitable jobs. Since I'm 11 years old, I'm glad some of the older bigger kids moved elsewhere. This 30 cents per round fee existed until 1936 when we caddies went on strike for 40 cents per 9 holes and 75 cents for 18 holes. I'll tell you more about this strike later.

Up until the spring of 1932, C.C. (Chris) Graves was the golf pro. Again, I'll tell you more about him later. A new golf pro, Homer Herpel, took over now and proceeded to organize the caddie program. He called each of us caddies into his office one at a time and took our names, addresses, ages and parent information. He would have taken phone numbers too, but I knew of no caddie who had one. I'm 12 years old and still very small but the caddie master is putting my name on the LINE UP sheet. In Mr. Herpel's office I was quite nervous. Since being small, I wasn't sure he too, might tell me to go home and eat some more biscuits. He was very kind and I answered his questions pretty well (I thought). For whatever reason, he gave me a B-class caddie badge, a three inch round white pin-on type with the number 72 on it in black letters. Also, it read "Rock Spring Caddie". Mr. Herpel instructed me to wear it at all times in the caddie yard and on the golf course. Heck, he didn't have to tell me that. I wore it everywhere. Even to mass on Sunday. Every caddie now wears a badge.

Since I'm still very small I still got passed up when my number 72 was at the top of the LINE UP sheet. Mostly because the golf bag I should have been assigned was judged to be too heavy or too big even though I was willing to drag that big bag around should they let me. Later that day I was given totes that were smaller and lighter.

1932 came and went and perhaps I caddied about 25 times. Now I'm frustrated to still be a B-class caddie. As I know I'm a better caddie than a good many A-class caddies.

Early in the summer of 1933 I had a heart to heart talk with the caddie master (Frank "Dump" Seibold) who had been very fair in assigning me totes. He was a good caddie previous to taking the caddie master job. He knew I was a pretty good caddie but told me Mr. Herpel would have to do the promoting. I volunteered to caddie for Mr. Herpel for free just to prove I was A-class stuff. Perhaps "Dump" had a talk with the pro about this as a few days later I was called in the golf shop (and my number 72 wasn't even at the top of the LINE UP sheet) and handed Mr. Herpel's golf bag.

At first I was a bit nervous on Number 1 tee. But it soon wore off and I became engrossed in this assignment. If I made any mistakes, I sure didn't notice 'em. When the round was over and I was returning Mr. Herpel's golf bag to the golf shop he was following me. When I took the bag off my shoulder, Mr. Herpel said to the caddie master, "Put this kid in the A-class." He paid me and tipped me a quarter. I couldn't get home fast enough to tell my Mom. She hugged me and reminded me, "See I told you you'd grow up some day." This day I grew seven feet tall.

All the frustrating years are behind me now and they don't pass up A-class caddies on the LINE UP sheets. ANOTHER PROUD DAY IN MY WORLD OF GOLF!

I'm hot stuff now. This marks the start of a new episode in my world of golf. At this time I'm 13 years old and it's 1933. The first year of caddying as a teenager. I left the caddie ranks as a 19 year old in 1939. So you see, I caddied all my teenage years and I invite you to come along and learn what a regular caddie did to earn a few nickels during the depression years of the 1930's.

The first objective for a caddie in those days was to make LINE UP and get an early number to insure a tote. To do this required getting out of bed at daybreak and hoofing it to the caddie yard. I can remember my mother not allowing me to leave the house for the LINE UP because it was still too dark outside on several occasions.

Saturdays, Sundays, and holidays were the big days for caddies. On these days in the summer months there were 30 to 45 caddies in the LINE UP. On Mondays and Tuesdays there were practically no caddies who were seen in the caddie yard before quarter to seven. Mondays were for golf for the caddies who cared to play. We were allowed to play from 7 a.m. 'till noon. When that Laclede Steel Mill whistle blew at high noon, those playing golf better not start another hole. The golf course maintenance superintendent was tough on kids playing golf after the whistle. He caught me a few times and the pro forbade me to play come next Monday. I learned to pay attention to the noon whistle. I loved playing golf and sneaked on the golf course many times when I thought it was safe. I got kicked off for a week or two a few times when I did get caught. If only they knew how much unauthorized golf I really played. Come to think of it, if I had a dime for every hole of such golf I probably could have bought a membership.

Tuesdays were Ladies' Day and they all took caddies. Usually 35 to 40 ladies teed it up this day. To make LINE UP this day wasn't necessary as we sometimes didn't have enough caddies for these gals. As a matter of fact, we occasionally got lectures from the pro when not enough caddies showed on Tuesday. The gals chewed on the pro and the pro chewed on the caddies. Nine o'clock a.m. was the starting time for the ladies to start golfing and yacking from Number 1 tee.

Wednesdays, Thursdays, and Fridays there were 15 to 25 caddies in the LINE UP. Other caddies appeared occasionally later and put their names at the bottom of the LINE UP sheet.

Weather played a big part in dictating just how many caddies got totes on any given day. Caddies analyzed their position fairly well as to whether or not they'd get a tote. As a matter of fact during the winter months when occasionally the sun was out and the temperature was pretty good and no snow on the course, several caddies showed on Saturdays and Sundays. The golf shop was closed but members brought their golf clubs with them. We pretty well knew the members who showed on these days. A couple of years I caddied in every month of the year.

THE LINE UP

I've been writing this word and perhaps some of you don't quite understand. LINE UP was at 7 a.m. each morning during the golf season. This was the time the caddie master showed and started to work. He didn't get off duty until the last golf bag was returned to the golf shop, usually about one hour after sundown. On his arrival, all the caddies present took part in policing the area around the club house, parking lot, and caddie yard. We picked up soda bottles, candy bar wrappers, and cigarette butts. Not too many cigarette butts as the caddies had already banged those that were over 3/4 of an inch long. Most of it was the mess we caddies made the previous day. About a 12 to 15 minute chore.

Then the caddie master lined us up in single file as we had arrived and put our names on the LINE UP sheet. The first name on the sheet got the tote of the first player needing a caddie. The second name got the second tote and so on down the line. When handed a tote, the caddie master checked your name off.

We caddies had some unwritten rules. We were allowed to trade positions in the LINE UP before the caddie master wrote up the LINE UP. Some kids had too early a number some days and afraid they'd get gypped before they could return to the caddie yard. They had other commitments that morning. Some cut grass, some had to help Dads, some had planned to swim, hike, etc. Several times I traded number 12 to 15 for numbers 1, 2, 3, 4, up to 10. You see only about 10 players or less played golf on week day mornings. When I traded numbers, I reasoned I'd get a morning tote. The number I gave up usually didn't require being in the caddie yard before noon. Sometimes morning toters got a second tote in the afternoon.

Once we showed for LINE UP we could leave when the caddie or caddies who would be behind you in the LINE UP showed. In other words if you were number 6, once number 7 showed, go ahead and leave but be back at 7 a.m. LINE UP.

There were several of us caddies who were Catholics and we arrived before 5:30 a.m. on Sundays. Other caddies allowed us to go to mass. We attended 6 a.m. mass at St. Anthony's Infirmary Chapel and 5:45 a.m. mass at St. Patrick's Church. We hoofed it to St. Anthony's about half a mile away and rode to St. Pat's one and a half miles away. Some of the caddies had ol' jalopies and some drove parent's cars on Sunday. We returned for the 7 a.m. LINE UP.

Then some kids left to go to Pie Town (upper Alton) and buy a sack of broken oatmeal cookies from a bakery up there. Then quite often these kids returned with a quart or two of milk. The milkman in those days made early morning deliveries to front porches. The bottles of milk mysteriously disappeared during the wee hours of the morning.

Once the caddie master completed putting our names on the LINE UP sheet, we were free to do most anything until time to get a tote. We had to be present when our name was called or we got "gypped". On a late arrival when we did show the caddies sounded off "YOU GOT GYPPED". Your name then went to the bottom of the LINE UP sheet. Most of the time you didn't get a tote that day.

There were lots of days caddies didn't get a tote and had arrived before 6 a.m. and were still in the caddie yard after sundown. Sometimes rain washed us out. And many are the times when say I was number 19 and only 18 players took caddies. This was a time I waited 'till a few minutes after sundown in hopes at least one more player would arrive. When I was convinced I'd not get a tote even though I'm number 1 now, I'd leave the caddie yard. Usually I'd not head straight home. My route home was along Number 9 where I'd hunt for golf balls or play a hole or two of golf. I usually got home before dark.

Being number 1 as I left this day meant nothing for tomorrow. A new LINE UP every day. Some weeks caddies were in the LINE UP five days and didn't get more than two totes. Too high a number or weather were the culprits. So that, my friends, was the LINE UP.

Before I tell you what caddies did from daybreak to LINE UP and how we spent time in and out of the caddie yard waiting for a tote, let me tell you that only a very few players carried their own golf clubs. We had one guy who played with only two clubs. He took a caddie. Easy tote as he carried one club and the caddie carried the other. In order for a player to get to Number 1 tee from either the golf shop or parking lot, he had to pass by the caddie yard. When he carried his own clubs as he passed the caddie yard, the caddies started a chant like a flock of baby chickens, "CHEAP, CHEAP, CHEAP". The chant was loud enough for him to hear and usually he got the message and on his next appearance took a caddie.

THE FUN CADDIES HAD AFTER
LINE UP

When LINE UP was over, we caddies were free to do most anything until our name was called for a tote. Since it's about 7:30 a.m. and with no Mom and Dad supervision, perhaps you'd like to know just what plans caddies made. None of whom need be in the caddie yard before 9 a.m. and most didn't need to worry of getting "gypped" until noon.

Some caddies had stricter parents than others and were instructed to return home immediately after LINE UP to return later. Several caddies lived two to three miles away and that would be quite a chore. Should one live three miles away and had to return home after LINE UP and get back by noon meant a six mile jaunt plus the three miles to make LINE UP, then another three miles after caddying. That's 12 miles of walking not including say 18 holes of bag toting (about seven miles). That's 19 miles! You can see why these caddies who lived that far away brought their lunches when arriving for LINE UP and stayed all day in the caddie yard. Or at least that's what their parents thought.

It's fun time as teenage boys plan a few hours of activity. Some went swimming. The Mississippi River, Blue Pool, Red Bridge, Big Arch, Black Creek are some of the swimming holes. Others planned to raid the peach orchard along Number 9 fairway. Some planned capturing a watermelon from a patch near Western Military Academy. Still others went for a hike up the bluffs of the Mississippi. As they went on this journey, they first took their flippers (slingshots), cut through Duncan Foundry scrap yard for a pocket full of half inch round punchings from quarter inch boiler plate (for ammunition) and stopped by Spark's Flour Mill to shoot pigeons. We also shot snakes on the bluffs. Quite often we kid's capped this adventure swimming in the Mississippi.

Many times we went golf ball hunting at both Rock and Muny. I'll tell you some stories on ball hunting later.

Other times we went crawdading (catching crawfish) and blue gill fishing in Western Military pond, at Big Arch, and Black Creek. Occasionally we had a fish fry. Some caddies went junking for old iron. They picked up all empty cigarette packs and saved the tin foils that were in them.

Sometimes we chose up sides and played softball or football.

Time of the year, day of the week, and weather dictated our choices. Yes, I'll admit I took part in most all of these activities at one time or another. As I reflect on my teenage years in the caddie yard and on the golf course, I'll have to say it was a real education.

Most all of us caddies went to school but several of us disappeared from the school yard at lunch time when a golf tournament was being held that afternoon and we knew we'd get to caddie that day. Sometimes we got to carry doubles (2 golf bags on the same round) as we were short on caddies. The pro knew what we were doing, but since he needed caddies, just winked at us. "Hooky" I believe they called it.

This day, the record book at school probably had us marked "FLUNKED", missing our formal arithmetic class where students learn 2+2=4. Well this day we were learning 2 willing feet + carrying 2 golf bags for 4 hours in the hot sun = 2 bucks. Now, who's to say which of these educations is best for a teenage boy earning bread for his destitute family.

Once the school truant officer showed at my house on one of these days and reported to my Mom that I wasn't in school that afternoon. When I did arrive home about 6:30 p.m., Mom was ready to climb my frame. That day I'd earned $2.00 and when I handed her a dollar she just grinned.

THE CADDIE BRIDGE

When caddies were arriving for LINE UP in the wee hours of the morning, we had to have a home plate or a home base. Since caddies were arriving from several directions, early on there were arguments and fist fights as to who got what numbers.

First of all we weren't allowed to congregate in the official caddie yard before LINE UP. They didn't want us caddies to start fires. It was very cold in the early mornings even in July and August. So we kids had our assembly just below the Rock Spring Caddie Yard in Rock Spring Park near a bridge over the creek that flows through the main picnic area of the park and near a burn pit. (Today, we call this a barbecue pit.) On cold mornings the first caddies to show, built a fire and we dragged park benches up to keep warm. This bridge was about 75 yards from the caddie yard and about 75 feet from the burn pit.

Caddies had an unwritten rule that as you arrived for a caddie number you had to cross the bridge from either direction. Upon arrival, when caddies got to within 100 yards of the bridge they could see other caddies coming from other directions. And then there were mad dashes to the bridge. Sometimes four caddies were coming from the south and five caddies coming from the north. Hey, it made a big difference for a tote if you were number 1 of this group or number 9. Caddies learned to run fast.

When I say caddies arrived in bunches, here is how this happened. Caddies knew where their caddie friends lived so this is how we came to arrive at the bridge in bunches. Say, for instance, two or three brothers left their homes together and their path was past my house. They'd holler, "Second Hand Man" or knock on my bedroom window. If I wasn't up yet (but usually I was), I'd jump into motion and catch up with them. We'd arrive at the caddie yard with perhaps another caddie or two.

This caddie bridge still exists today. It has concrete side walls about 30 inches high and about 16 inches thick on either side and they look the same now as in the 1930s. We caddies used this bridge for several other purposes. We did some crawdading (our term for catching crawfish) from it. We also shot at rats with flippers from it as a garbage pit was near the bridge. We once had a long rope (about 100 feet long about 1 inch in diameter). We stretched it along the roadway over the bridge between the concrete side walls. Then we'd choose up sides and play TUG-OF-WAR. The object was to pull the opposite team across the bridge. On mild weather mornings we sat on the side walls. You might then see 15 to 20 caddies sometimes lined up on the side walls.

We also used the bridge for new caddie initiations. I'll tell you about this later.

Since the caddies sat around the fire for as long as two hours before LINE UP, we played many games. This burn pit was in the main picnic area. Many of us brought potatoes from home, coated them with mud and put them in the hot coals. And we caught large crawfish in the creek and boiled the tails and pincers. We had several such feasts. Baked potatoes and miniature lobster for breakfast. And you thought only kings dined in such a manner.

I've already told of breakfast of broken oatmeal cookies and milk.

Some caddies were crack shots with flippers and killed birds that we cleaned and roasted. As a caddie, I've eaten dove, pigeon, blackbird, chicken, robin, and a few more. Robin is delicious but don't tell the game warden or the Audubon Society.

Occasionally two caddies captured a chicken. Get this. Number 2 hole at Rock is bordered by Salu Street or a better description would be Salu Road. It was a dirt road that connected middletown to Upper Alton. Only two houses existed on this road along the section that bordered the golf course during my caddie days. One lady who lived in one of those two houses had chickens. They were not penned and would feed along the hedgerow that was on the opposite side of the road from the golf course.

In plotting to capture a chicken, here is what two caddies would do. First they used a blue gill fishing line. (We bought a few at Woolworths for a dime). This consisted of 12 feet of green cotton line, a lead sinker crimped to it just above a small blue gill hook. They baited the hook with a kernel of corn and strung the line though the hedgerow. Now the trap is set. With a hand full of corn, one caddie throws it in the area of the baited hook and says, "Here chickie, here chickie". The chickens start gobbling up the corn. When the chicken gets the kernel on the hook, the other caddie reels it through the hedgerow in the same manner you'd reel in a fish. By this time the corn throwing caddie is in a position to grab the chicken and choke it to death without making a disturbance to alert the chicken's owner. Caddies then picked it, dressed it, and roasted it in "wild west style".

Caddies are always hungry and made several trips to peach orchards, apple, pear, and plum trees. There also was a grape arbor in the vicinity that got regular visits from the caddies.

CADDIE INITIATIONS

They varied from time to time. Pantsing a caddie was one. A group of caddies would hold a new caddie while others removed his pants and shorts. Then they'd hang 'em up in a tree and he'd have to climb to get 'em back, bare from the waist down. Sometimes when a picnic was in progress these pants were put in an area near the picnickers and again the initiated caddie had to go retrieve them with a bare bottom while the other caddies made sure the picnickers viewed the show.

Another initiation was the paddle machine. Whereas caddies lined up single file about five feet apart and had their legs and feet far apart. The initiated caddie had to go through the whole line (sometimes 30 caddies) on his hands and knees and through each one's legs. As he passed under each caddie, he got swatted on the butt. The longer he lingered the more he got swatted.

Later on we had an initiation we caddies called "Deliver Unto Me The Black Baloney". It went this way. The new caddie was conned into playing what the caddies told him was the easy part. He was the "king". And the throne was the west end of one of the caddie bridge side walls. He sat on the throne. A veteran caddie played the part of the bandit named "Black Baloney" who was to go hide in the park and a posse of six or eight caddies were sent to capture him. All the caddies, except the new kid, knew where Black Baloney was. (Up the creek making mud balls for he and the posse. And of course out of sight of the king.) The posse returned with Black Baloney in the lead with his right hand behind his back holding a mud ball out of sight. Each member of the posse had his left hand on the shoulder of the caddie in front of him and the right hand behind his back holding a mud ball. Now they proceeded to lead Black Baloney before the king. At such time, the caddies who did not take part as a member of the posse instructed the king to shout, "Deliver Unto Me the Black Baloney!" And with that he got bombarded with the mud balls. The king got muddy and lots of laughs and was now officially initiated to the Rock Spring Caddie Ranks.

THE CADDIE YARD, ROCK SPRINGS PARK, AND GAMES WE PLAYED WITH PICNICKERS

The Rock Spring C.C. clubhouse was built on the top of a hill bordering the main picnic area of Rock Spring Park. The parking lot was cut into the side of the hill along the south side of the clubhouse. The caddie yard was just over the retaining wall of the parking lot and still a bit closer to view activity of the picnickers for the caddies.

Now, understand, in the 1930s, Rock Spring Park was a bee hive of activity. So much so that there was always a concession stand operating during the summer months. In my days the Patterson boys, Harold and Russell worked this stand. It was a small building, approximately 12 feet by 12 feet. When opened, three sides lifted up to accommodate customers from the three sides. Caddies spent much of their earnings on popsicles, ice cream, frozen Snickers, Milky Ways, and cold sodie. (Caddie language for soda pop.)

In these days, the park had a night watchman. In the 1930s he was Dode Daley, an uncle to my caddie friend "Whitey" Hamilton. He was a tough bird and kept law and order in the park. He came on shift at 7:00 p.m. and didn't leave the park until 7:00 am. From time to time, we caddies gave him fits. In those early mornings before LINE UP, we caddies congregated about 150 yards from the spot he was parked and usually asleep at this time in his Model A Ford Coupe. He made periodic trips through the park in his Model A. He packed a gun and allowed no loitering in the park after dark. He was known to stick his .45 into loiterers' ribs and say "get going".

In the park was a pavilion for band concerts, dances and other picnic activities, a baseball diamond, three playground areas with swings, teeter totters, sand boxes, several horse shoe pits, two restrooms for males and two for ladies and seven drinking fountains.

Alton had street cars in those days and the Middle Town Line had a stop at the park entrance. This Middle Town Line ran from downtown Alton to Forkeyville (a term for an area just beyond the eastern city limits, just a quarter mile short of Alton State Mental Hospital) Earlier this street car once ran all the way to the hospital. Since there were very few automobiles in those days, the street cars got lots of play. Adults could ride for a dime and kids four cents. Several street car lines crisscrossed the city and a passenger was able to transfer from one line to another. So you see it was possible to get to Rock Spring Park by street car from almost any point in the city. The street cars were scheduled to run every 20 minutes. Some caddies rode them. Those who lived near Watertower Playground on State Street (about three miles from the caddie yard).

At times when the weather was ideal, the stop the street car made at the park, unloaded two or more families with kids and picnic baskets every 20 minutes.

Sometimes three to six families joined at picnic tables. There were church groups, etc. Some groups brought picnic baskets full of sandwiches and goodies of all kinds. We caddies watched those picnic tables very carefully from our bird's eye view from the caddie yard.

Should picnickers leave the immediate area of the picnic tables to play games and such, and left the goodies unguarded, caddies made mad dashes past these tables, faking a running game, and grabbed something to eat: an apple, a sandwich, a piece of cake, etc.

Another trick (or game) caddies played with picnickers went like this. Caddies watched them sitting, eating at meal times from the caddie yard. Some caddies' mouths were watering for the fried chicken that they reasoned was more than this table could eat. A couple of caddies would test the situation. At the proper time (when they judged the picnickers had enough and some kids had already gotten up from the table and went swinging, etc.), they would mosey past the picnic table loaded with leftovers. Several picnickers were still sitting yacking. These caddies with expressions and actions (without talking) appear interested and hungry. It was a sympathy tactic. Many are the times, a picnicker would invite these caddies by saying something like this, "Hungry kids? Help yourself." And they did. Other caddies usually followed and several times eight to ten caddies got a feast!

Then another trick was to pass by the picnic table as the picnickers were preparing to leave and picking up the leftovers. Several times caddies were invited to take whatever leftovers they wanted. I've seen 'em bring boxes of sandwiches, half a cake, and half a watermelon back to the caddie yard. Why is it caddies are always hungry?

GOLF BALL HUNTING

You've heard how we kids waded a small shallow pond behind Number 7 green and retrieved several golf balls that we sold for nickels and dimes and bought penny candy and five cent soda pops. Those were the days, prior to my first caddie assignment in 1928. We also hunted balls along the hedgerow of Number 9 and along Salu Road where balls bounced out of bounds from holes 2, 5, 6, and 8.

As a youngster trying to get a tote, just hanging around the caddie yard was educational. Number 1 tee was next to the caddie yard and I'd watch the players' tee shots. Some balls went in the creek, some out of bounds right, some in heavy rough left. On many occasions balls hit to these areas were not retrieved and I'd run down and try to find 'em and many, I did.

As I got to be nine, ten, and eleven years old, I still only got to caddie when they ran out of regular caddies. Many are the times I earned more finding and selling golf balls than had I caddied.

Hanging around the caddie yard and with big ears, I was learning most of the members' names and I knew them by sight and the cars they drove. Back in those days members drove Mormans, LaSalles, Moons, Essexs, Pierce-Arrows, Packards, Hubmobiles, and Studebakers. And then there were Fords, Chevys,

Dodges, and Buicks too. The C.C. pro (Chris Graves) drove a car called a Eureka. I've never seen another to this day.

Almost 50% of the members had their names stamped on their golf balls. There was a device on the back counter of the golf shop for this purpose. For $1.25, a member bought a die with his name on it. A rack held these dies in alphabetical order. In those days, most all golf balls were bought in the golf shop and usually by a sleeve of three. The caddie master or pro, in selling a member a sleeve of balls, would take his die from the rack and stamp his name on them.

At a tender age, I quickly learned members would not buy used balls with some other member's name on them. As a matter of fact, early on, I didn't feel right about selling balls I'd found with members' names on them. I thought God would get me if I didn't return it to the original owner or take it to the golf shop.

I did take a few to the golf shop and got only a "thanks". Then I discussed this with a Catholic priest and I can remember to this day his exact words. When I told him, "I don't feel right when I find a ball with a member's name on it and I keep it to sell." He said, "the golfer who lost the ball is playing a game whereas he is taking a chance of losing it. Once he's given it up for lost, it becomes anybody's ball. It's a nice act of charity should you return it, but it's not your responsibility. However should you find a billfold, wrist watch or some other personal item, then that's a different story." That I knew and would do.

I then became more aggressive in hunting and selling golf balls. Here's a trick I learned when I found a golf ball with a member's name stamped on it. Let's say I found a golf ball stamped "R.F. RADECKE". I knew who Mr. Radecke was but he didn't know I knew. I'd seek him out on the golf course. (Usually at Number 4 tee 'cause it's kinda hidden from view of the rest of the golf course.) And with three golf balls in my hand, one of which is stamped with his name positioned where he can easily read it, I'd say, "Do you want to buy a ball, mister?" Usually he'd say to his fellow competitor as he looks at the balls, "Look, this kid has one with my name on it." (Like it's a coincidence.) I'm laughing inside. And he adds, "What do you want for it, kid?" Early on, I'd say "a dime". But I soon wised up and would ask 15 cents and usually got it. Some gave me a quarter.

I pulled this little sales gimmick so many times that members who lost the most balls knew I knew them. Not only that but some would tell me where they'd lost a ball. They would say something like this, "I knocked a brand new Kroflite in 'deep water' (a section in the creek so named) and if you find it, I'll give you a quarter." Or they might offer to tell me, "I knocked my drive out of bounds into the hedgerow on Number 2. It was a Spalding DOT. Find it and it's worth a quarter to you." Or , I've had them say, "My drive off Number 9 tee hit in the big sycamore tree on a fly and we couldn't find it. I'll buy it if you find it. It was a Worthington Sweet Shot with my name on it."

When I became a regular caddie, I spent lots of time hunting golf balls. There's always idle time waiting for a tote and I'd use much of this time in the creek and woods and out of bounds on Number 1.

We caddies hunted the whole course some days. Other days, we journeyed to Muny (Alton Municipal Golf Course). We sold balls we'd found at Rock and we hunted Muny too. Muny players weren't as picky as members of Rock. They'd buy balls with Rock members' names on them. They didn't care.

As youngsters, we learned little tricks to make the balls look more attractive to the buyer. Whenever we could, we'd present these balls wet as they shine better. Of course we removed all dirt, mud, tree marks, etc. as best we could. We always washed these balls and got the grass stains off 'em.

The three golf courses in the area all had tee boxes at each tee. They were wooden structures about 36" high, 30" long, and 16" wide and mounted on four legs. Picture an orange crate with four legs or a double drain sink. This tee box had two compartments approximately 16" by 15" and 16" deep. Now if you stand at a double drain sink and the two compartments are these dimensions, you pretty well got the picture. In one compartment was an eight quart galvanized bucket of water. The other compartment was filled with white sand. These tee boxes were painted white and had the hole number, yardage, and par stenciled on the side. The tee box on Number 1 at Rock read, "No. 1 400 yds. PAR 4".

These tee boxes not only were there to identify the holes, but they had a two fold purpose. First, by moistening the sand with the water the player built a sand tee for his drive. (They didn't have wooden tees in those days.) Then the sand acted as a grit and with clear water, the caddies were able to wash golf balls. The little wooden pegs (tees) came later. As a matter of fact the first tees were made of celluloid. They were made in two pieces: the head that held the ball and the stem that was pushed into the ground. These two pieces were so made that the stem fit up into the head and was glued in.

These tee boxes disappeared in the late 1930s. It was a chore to replace the buckets of water each day. The sand, too, had to be replaced periodically as birds with their nasty habits were attracted to fresh water and sand.

Getting back to ball hunting....

Many are the times we had pockets full of balls and had already approached all the potential buyers and sold some. Sometimes we'd ditch a dozen or so balls. Here's how we usually did this. In the shade of a tree, we'd take our pocket knives and cut a square of turf about nine inches square. Then we'd dig a hole deep enough to hold the balls then cover it over with dirt and turf. Never did anyone else find this type hiding place.

Hunting and selling golf balls was big business to my caddie friends and I. We not only went on many golf ball hunting expeditions, but found many ways of selling them. Many are the times I've bought a golf ball from another caddie for a nickel that I judged to be worth a dime to a quarter after I'd clean it up and knew where to sell it. Caddies who were willing to sell these to me were more interested in converting this ball to a candy bar, sodie, or popsicle than holding on to it. As I've said, "caddies are always hungry."

We had some ball buying customers who lived within a mile radius of the caddie yard. We'd occasionally knock on the door with golf balls we judged they'd buy. Some Muny golfers had favorite balls and they told us to save those for them. The near perfect ones brought a quarter.

We had a source for selling balls that we had a hard time selling at golf courses. There was Black's Grocery Store on Humbert St. between Salu St. and Pohattan St. Mr. Bill Black operated this store. He bought all the golf balls we could bring him that had no cuts in the cover for five cents in trade. Not only did he buy from Rock Spring caddies, but from Muny caddies as well as from neighborhood kids. This store was about a mile from the caddie yard. Occasionally we caddies pooled the balls we had (sometimes as many as 30) and took them to Mr. Black and traded them for a chunk of baloney and a loaf of bread. Right now, I can taste that good Luer's Packing House Baloney. (Luer's was once a slaughter house and meat packing company located in Alton.) Their meats were second to none especially their wieners and baloney.

Mr. Black put these balls in a cardboard box and resold them to golfers for a dime. Take your pick. I bought a few for a dime; those I judged I could resell for 15 cents to a quarter. The balls Mr. Black couldn't sell to golfers, he sold for five cents each to a driving range operator who repainted and striped them for driving range use.

In dealing with Mr. Black, he didn't care if the ball was white, black or brown just so it had no cuts. A golf ball that lies in water or a mud bank too long will get brown and eventually black as the ace of spades. This only destroys the cosmetics and makes them unattractive to the buyer.

It's surprising how many golfers think these balls are water soaked or dead. Nothing could be farther from the truth. Color means nothing as to how a golf ball performs. And of course no water can penetrate it if the cover is intact. I learned as a ten year old that balls black as the ace of spaces traveled off the golf club face as well as ones right out of the cellophane.

Here's a personal theory of mine and I challenge anyone to prove me wrong. "A golf ball resting on the bottom of a deep lake is better preserved than in your golf bag or golf shop shelf." Now you're saying, "How come you think that?" First of all, a golf ball is basically a rubber product. So are automobile tires. Tire manufacturers instruct those selling tires to store them in a cool, dark place to best preserve quality and avoid deterioration. What natural place more qualifies than a cave or a deep lake?

The culprit most responsible for deteriorating a golf ball is the rise and fall of temperatures which is the case no matter where your golf bag goes. Usually it spends lots of time in the trunk of your car. And that's the worst place for your golf clubs and balls. Temperatures in it get to 200 degrees and more should you park in the sunlight when it's 90 degrees in the shade. I've seen many cases of golfers showing me golf balls that were stored in the car trunk for long periods. Some exploded, some the covers popped off, some got egg shaped. Several have shown me golf clubs that because of these heat exposures, the club heads became loosened.

For even temperature, the bottom of a deep lake remains about 55 degrees: ideal for preserving golf balls. Another factor to be considered is the influence gravity has on a golf ball. A golf ball almost floats. So, as it rests on the bottom of a lake, it's almost like an astronaut in space: nearly weightless. Now, perhaps, you're saying, "What does that mean?" It means the pressure around the circumference of the ball is constant. Whereas a ball resting on a shelf (as in a golf shop or your golf bag) is subject to gravity trying to push it down. Should this ball remain on a shelf in the same position for any length of time, it will develop a small flat spot. This perhaps is a bit technical and may have little to do with how a golf ball rolls on the green. But nevertheless, it's a factor proven in physics and logic.

So take a tip from an ol' golf ball hawk. Buying used golf balls is usually your best buy.

I've just mentioned how a golf ball rolls on the green. Would you be surprised if I told you over 99% of all golf balls are out of balance? I'll do a chapter on this subject later and I'll tell you how I test balls and how Mr. C.C. (Chris) Graves (the pro at Rock until 1932) tested golf balls he used.

Golf ball hunting is very hazardous and there's a big difference in looking for golf balls and "hunting" golf balls. The lookers pass up too many as they usually avoid briars, poison ivy and heavy weeded areas. Hunters cover the whole area. Oh yeah, we knock spiders off our faces running into spider webs with our eyes glued on the ground. We get stung by bees and wasps. Hornets, too are a problem though I've never been stung by one. But I've had lots of bee and wasp stings. Briars have cut me up something awful and have caused tears in my clothing. Poison ivy wasn't a problem for me but was to several of my caddie friends.

Snakes are another hazard. On one ball hunting expedition with my friend Robert (Bones) Pace, he stepped on a garter snake and it bit him! Bones had no ill effects of this bite. I once stepped on a black snake while running barefoot. Once while hunting golf balls I walked upon a coiled copperhead snake. I was alone and on my way to the caddie yard and my route was along Number 9 hole. I went into the woods and was following a small narrow path (probably made by a small rabbit). This path became two paths. Picture the letter Y. This coiled snake was positioned in the crutch of the Y and looking up the single path as I was proceeding toward the snake. Apparently the snake was hunting and was expecting a small rabbit would be along. It wasn't expecting me nor was I expecting it. I didn't see the snake until I was but one step away from it. I froze. Never in my life have I been more frightened. Now I was faced with a decision. Should I try to ease back and let the snake alone while thinking the moment I move the snake will strike? Or should I kick at it and hope for the best? I elected to back off very, very carefully and let the snake alone while I hurried back home to change my underwear. I've told this story several times and have been told that it wasn't a copperhead. There were rumors of copperheads in that area during this time. All I know was it was a large shiny brown snake and it didn't show me it's I.D. so we'll never know it's true identity.

It was a lesson for me as from then on I carried a golf club or tree branch and fanned the weeds in front of me to scare off these reptiles. With this method, I've flushed quail, pheasants, and rabbits. They scare hell out of you too.

My caddie friend Hobart (Hub) Turley found a dead body while looking for a golf ball his player knocked in a wooded creek area along Number 9. Only a short distance from the copperhead location. This was the body of the Alton High School janitor who had apparently committed suicide.

Creeks, ponds, and lakes on or bordering golf courses are very good places to wade and swim for golf balls. Since we waded most of the time barefoot, sharp objects were obstacles. Broken bottles and tin cans gave us many cuts to our feet.

Muny had a pond between Number 3 tee and Number 3 green. We caddies got in it periodically. If we were caught in that pond, the maintenance supervisor would take us to the police station. This only happened to Rock caddies once. I wasn't one of them.

When we were going to get in this pond, three or four caddies would be on this expedition. One caddie served as a lookout while the others waded. The lookout laid on his belly at the crest of the hill overlooking the pond where he had a good view of golfers playing Number 2, the clubhouse, and maintenance shed. Floyd M. was the greens keeper, maintenance foreman, etc. and was a tough bird. When the lookout hollers, "Floyd is coming", we grabbed our shoes and quickly got out of bounds and hid in Logan's cornfield. He never did catch our gang.

We got in Cloverleaf Golf Course Lake a few times. Older caddies told stories of going to Cloverleaf late in the night to capture balls from that lake. Oh, if I only had some of the golf balls from the 1930s now. Some of them are worth $600 to collectors. But of course, if I had the penny gum baseball cards I had in those days, I'd be worth a fortune. We kids had stacks of them and traded each other. I once had 25 Babe Ruths (worth several thousand dollars today) and God knows how many Lou Gehrig, Jimmy Foxx, Hack Wilson, Bill Dickey, and almost all National and American League ball players of the late 1920s and 1930s. My Mom pitched them all once I reached the age when my interest in girls became more important.

Since I still hunt golf balls today and have been for nearly 70 years, if I had all of them in a pile, I'd need a box car to contain them.

60

GOLF PROFESSIONALS AT ROCK SPRINGS C.C.

There were only three golf professionals in my caddie days at Rock. Mr. C.C. (Chris) Graves was the pro the day I first caddied in 1928.

In the early years of the 1920s, a golf professional was considered a servant and had little social life with the members. He was hired to be greens keeper, supervise the golf course maintenance, run the golf shop, build and repair golf clubs, give golf lessons, and manage the caddie program. As a matter of fact, the golf shop was isolated from the rest of the clubhouse. To get to the golf shop from any clubhouse location, you had to go outside and down a flight of steps (about 25) which were on both east and west ends of the huge traditional clubhouse.

The golf shop, repair shop, and furnace room were on the parking lot level. It actually was the basement of the clubhouse.

Mr. Graves came here from Scotland where he learned his golf skills. He was 50ish in 1928. He was small in stature: about 5 feet 1 inch and had to be soaking wet to weigh 125 pounds. A tough bird for us caddies but fair. We caddies referred to him as the "little general" in our circles. But we addressed him "Mr. Graves". The members called him "Chris".

Mr. Graves was pro in 1928, '29, '30, and '31, my first four years (of trying to be accepted as a caddie).

At playing golf, Mr. Graves was unique. He was the straightest driver. His drives weren't long (average about 225 yards) but straight down the middle. He could thread a needle with his brassie (No. 2 wood) and spoon (No. 3 wood) and was an excellent chipper and putter. Though he was right handed, he could also play left handed. He sometimes had bets where he played one handed. Believe me, he collected on 90% of his golf bets with the members while playing right, left, or one handed. I remember one veteran caddie commenting on Mr. Graves' golf game. He said, "Mr. Graves never lost a golf ball." In all probability that's not true but never lost but a few.

Mr. Graves took a liking to me. Of course trying to be accepted as a caddie, I used some brown nose tactics. When he was working in his repair shop, I'd look through the window and watch him work. He would invite me in and showed me how to use some tools and showed me how to fit a hickory shaft in an iron head and other golf club repairs.

One thing I remember about Mr. Graves was how he handled caddies. He was strict and was tough on horseplay. When Mr. Graves saw two caddies fist fighting he'd come out to the caddie yard. At his appearance the fight usually broke up. But when it didn't, he'd watch for a minute or two and then break it up. Made the two fighting caddies shake hands and bought both a bottle of pop. In most cases these two caddies became good friends.

Mr. Graves was an excellent teacher. He taught the basic fundamentals of the golf swing. As I reflect on his method to swing a golf club, he was a classic example of how simple the golf swing really is. And he could demonstrate to pupils by hitting golf balls both right and left handed.

After Mr. Graves left the post as Rock Spring Golf Professional, he built a driving range two miles out of town on Route 140. My best golf competitor and caddie friend, Hobart (Hub) Turley and I hit balls there quite often. Mr. Graves gave us many golf tips. Since both Hub and I won Alton City Golf Championships in different years, much of what Mr. Graves taught us was responsible.

On this story I must tell you. My first of back to back city championships was in the summer of 1941. Mr. Graves is in a small gallery as I played the 36 hole final. My opponent was the defending champion, Bill Usinger. In the morning 18 hole round I had Bill four down after 14 holes. Then I started shanking the ball (hitting it partly on the hosel) and lost the next four holes. This makes Bill and I go to lunch all even in the match. Before I started the afternoon 18, Mr. Graves told me what I was doing to shank the ball and how to correct it. Golfers know the shanks are not easy to cure. I went out and won the Alton City Championship beating Bill three and two. Thank you, Mr. Graves, wherever you are.

Mr. Graves passed away about 40 years ago.

While I'm on the subject, there are two words golfers use that start with SH. Shank is one of them. Using them, you're golf cursing. Other golf curse words are yip and choke. Caddies called a "shank" a snap fade.

In 1932, Mr. Homer Herpel took over as golf professional. Earlier in this book, I told you how he first organized the caddie program and assigned caddie badges to us. To me he put me down as a B-class caddie and the next year promoted me to A-class caddie.

Mr. Herpel was on this assignment for three years: '32, '33, and '34. He was an excellent golfer and teacher. Had a classic golf swing. He toured Rock Spring golf course methodically, shooting 34, 35, 36 with monotonous regularity. And often shot 32 and 33.

He came here from a pro job in St. Louis, Missouri. He somewhat mumbled as he talked. The caddies immediately jumped on this frailty by nick naming him "mush mouth".

As a caddie, I shagged balls when he was giving golf lessons many times. That was an assignment the caddie master would give me as a B-class caddie. It paid 25 cents plus tips. About an hour job.

On these ball shagging details (lessons and practice sessions), I'd take with me a baseball glove. We were expected to run down each ball as it was hit. I'd catch some on the fly, some on a bounce, and some bad bounces caught me on the kisser. God, those balls are hard.

Mr. Herpel did lots of practice swinging. The thing I most remember about this man was how he took practice swings before starting a round of golf. He positioned himself so his shadow would be cast in front of him. He'd know his club position at the top of his backswing and could tell if his head was moving. If the shadow moved of course, the head was moving. Some caddies thought he spent too much time doing this as they'd say "Look, Mush mouth is admiring his form." This shadow watching is a very good tip. All of us should use it.

After leaving this Rock Spring assignment, he went back to St. Louis. I didn't see him again until sometime in the late 1940s. He and I were in the gallery of a local St. Louis tourney. I went up to him and asked if he remembered me. He didn't recognize me from sight and I didn't expect him to. But when I told him my name and that I had been a caddie when he was pro at Rock, he said, "Sure I remember you. You were a fine caddie." And I replied, "I'll always remember you as promoting me to A-class caddie as a 13 year old."

Mr. Herpel had a daughter who was once one of the best female players in St. Louis. I don't know what happened to Mr. Mush Mouth or his daughter.

In the fall of 1934, Lou Miller took over as pro at Rock. Lou came here from a pro job in Bloomington, Illinois. Lou was once a caddie at Rock but it was before my time in the caddie yard. Lou did more for us caddies than the other two professionals. Having been a caddie, perhaps he knew of the mischief caddies got into while waiting for a tote. He got us softballs and bats, horse shoes, and organized the annual caddie banquet.

He too was a fine player. As a matter of fact, I told him, "You ought to be on the tour". That was 1936 and he said, "You really think so?" My comment was after I'd caddied for him when he shot a pair of 32s. Then I said, "Those guys on tour couldn't beat the 64 you shot today." He laughed and handed me a quarter tip. (I told you caddies had the smarts of a business man.)

"Uncle Louie" was the nickname the caddies planted on him. Perhaps because two of his young nephews visited him quite often in the golf shop. They addressed him as "Uncle Lou". He was known to be real close with a buck. But he did tip his caddies well.

"Uncle Louie" had us caddies doing all kind of chores for him. We weeded greens when needed. He let us play golf as pay. When his car needed washing, he paid us by letting us play golf. I remember riding with him to his mother's house on Alby Street and I cut her lawn while he ate lunch. I got to play 18 holes of golf for this chore.

Since I was interested in playing golf and Lou knew this, he conned me into doing quite a few small jobs for 18 holes of golf.

Once I was kicked off for a week. I was caught playing unauthorized golf. But I was still hanging around the caddie yard. Under those circumstances I got a little more aggressive hunting and selling balls. Even my mom didn't know I was "kicked off". Some days I earned more than had I caddied.

The fourth day of that "kicked off" week, they ran out of caddies so I went to Lou and asked forgiveness. Since he needed caddies he said, "okay" and gave me a sermon that went something like this, "Dog gone it, Mike, you kids get me in trouble when members see you playing on the greens." To which I responded, "Okay, Mr. Miller but I won't do it anymore." Both of us knew I was lying.

Later I worked for Lou as assistant caddie master. I worked one summer on Fridays when the regular caddie master had his day off. Since this job paid only one dollar, I also got the privilege to caddie for most anyone and play golf most any evening. On this job I also helped the regular caddie master, Ray Knapp, clean and polish golf clubs. Lou and Ray were an excellent team. Both were together yet as pro and caddie master at Rock when I went in the service in 1942. Ray and I played golf several evenings after the shop closed.

CADDIE MASTERS FROM 1928 TO 1939

Here is a list of caddie masters. The first name was on duty in 1928 and the second followed him and then right on down the line. I can't remember the exact year that each came and went as caddie masters.

1. Harry Curry
2. Frank (Hammie) Hamilton
3. Joe Donelson
4. Frank (Dump) Seibold
5. Roland Orr
6. Joe Wright
7. Ray Knapp

All of these caddie masters were former caddies. Most of these guys were 18 to 21 years old and since they were in contact with members who held positions in local industry, they often got jobs at Western Cartridge, Alton Box Board, Owen Illinois Glass, Laclede Steel, Illinois Terminal Railroad, and others. They were given jobs. Usually the pro encouraged this in late autumn when golf slowed up and he had to let go of his help.

Members had favorite caddies and those in position to get you hired, would do so when jobs opened up. Remember, it's the depression years. Things started to open up in the late 1930s and the older caddies went to work in industry.

Through caddying, I got my first real job in September of 1939. I caddied for a Mr. Lafayette Young who was general manager of Laclede Steel and he put me to work there. I got the opportunity to serve a machinist apprenticeship. I remember the day I went to work. There were some 300 men at the Laclede Steel main gate once they heard "Laclede is hiring". When I was called to come through the gate, one big strapping man said, "Look, they're putting a baby to work." At that time, I'm 19 years old and weighed 119 pounds and still growing. Some food for thought: my pay was 45 cents an hour. We worked a 44 hour week. Five eight hour shifts and four hours on Saturday at time and a half. Forty hours @ 45 cents = $18.00. Four hours @ time and a half = $2.70. So you see, I earned $20.70 a week. I never made LINE UP again. But I did visit the caddie yard quite often and would caddie if I was needed after all caddies had a tote. My caddie friends called me "$20.00 a week millionaire".

The four hour shift on Saturdays was from 7 a.m. till 11 a.m.. After showering, I'd head for the regular 1 o'clock, 15 cent skins game at Muny.

One caddie master Frank (Hammie) Hamilton moved to the locker room and he held this job until going in the service in 1942. This locker room attendant job was considered quite lucrative as he got many tips. "Hammie" kept the members' golf shoes shined, tended bar, and kept the locker room spick and span.

"Hammie" was killed on Okinawa in World War II.

Frank (Dump) Seibold was killed in Germany in the same war.

Roland Orr took a job on the golf course. He cut greens, etc. Later he was given a job at Laclede Steel Company. He and I worked a bit together there.

Joe Donelson came out and joined us caddies for golf on Mondays after he took Laclede employment. He was a fine player. Won the city championship once. At the time, he played 10 cent skins games with us. He was violating the rules. In order to play golf on Monday mornings, caddies had to have caddied in the previous seven days. But they weren't all that tough on this rule. As a matter of fact, Herb Miller who was a brother to the pro Lou Miller, also played some Mondays with us. Of course his brother didn't care. Herb worked shift work at Shell Oil Company and played when his work didn't interfere. Herb lived in Upper Alton and come Monday 7 a.m., here comes Herb packing a set of golf clubs through the park to Number 1 tee. We caddies enjoyed having Herb join our skins game as he let us use his clubs too. Those were the years of '37, '38, and '39. I'm 17, 18, and 19 years old.

Without Herb, we caddies played with a mismatched set of clubs. Most of us had a club or two. Only one bag. It would contain three or four drivers and three or four putters and a few other clubs. Sometimes we played an eightsome. When eight agreed to play dime skins. But usually five or six caddies were in this group.

Here's how we caddies played. Like I said, usually it was a five or sixsome. With one golf bag we drove from Number 1 tee and the shortest drive carried the bag. And it was his responsibility to carry it to the next tee. In this case to Number 2 tee. The highest score on Number 1 carried the bag on hole Number 2. In most cases there were ties for this honor. The ties then drove from Number 2 tee. The shortest drive carried and he wasn't relieved of this chore 'till Number 3 tee. We proceeded with this format the whole round.

Let me tell you a story about one of these driving contests to carry the bag. One Monday five of us caddies had tied for high score on Number 9. That meant the bag carrier on Number 9 carried to Number 1 tee to start the second nine.

There was a slight tail wind this day as I was first to tee it up. I cracked one over the creek and even with the wagon bridge, 250 yards. With this drive, I was confident all four of these caddies couldn't knock one past me. Guess who carried the bag on Number 1? Me. These other caddies were Hobart (Hub) Turley, Jesse (the Judge) Pace, John (King Rope) Beneze, and Walter (Schnoz) Calvey. This group called me "Short Hitter" the rest of the round.

Getting back to caddie masters. They worked long hours from 7 a.m. LINE UP until an hour after sundown. Twelve to thirteen hours of duty. They showed rain or shine six days a week. Since all of these guys were ex-caddies, they knew most all members by name, sight, and the cars they drove. They recognized the playing members by the golf bag and clubs. They didn't need to pay attention to the bag tags and they knew the pigeon hole each member had for storing his or her golf bag.

A caddie master's job was to keep the members' clubs cleaned and buffed, keep the caddies in line, serve up candy bars and soda pop, and act as assistant to the pro.

His job also required answering the phone. The calls that came in originated in the golf shop and the caddie master transferred the call to other locations. Quite often emergency calls came in for doctors. Say, for instance, an emergency call came in for Dr. McGinnis. The caddie master would send a caddie to call him in off the golf course. I had that chore many times.

Caddie masters had their own way of putting caddies names on the LINE UP SHEET. Some used full names, some used an initial for first name and spelled out the last name. Others just put down caddie nicknames and still, when Mr. Herpel gave us badge numbers, for awhile, caddie masters put down numbers only.

Numbers and nicknames caused some confusion. However, once when using nicknames, the LINE UP read something like this:

No. 1   Dog Patch
No. 2   Bite-The-Dust
No. 3   Bones
No. 4   Hollywood
No. 5   King Rope
No. 6   War Pants
No. 7   Schnoz
No. 8   Shoe Polish
No. 9   Jeep
No. 10   Wheeze
No. 11   Pistol
No. 12   Cotton Top
No. 13   Root
No. 14   Bright-In-Spots

No. 15   Gramma
No. 16   Grampa
No. 17   Hoot, The Owl
No. 18   Judge
No. 19   Hub
No. 20   Brownie

Yes, all of these were caddie nicknames. Both caddies and caddie masters recognized caddies by nicknames.

I've mentioned nicknames we caddies had for the golf pros and some other personnel around the golf course and clubhouse. One maintenance supervisor snitched on us for playing golf. We called him "Cliff, the Snitch". Rock had a maintenance worker who just winked at us when he saw us playing golf. He was Cal Garrett. We caddies called him "Cal the Pal".

We caddies had nicknames for some members too but I'd rather not go into that as some weren't fit for print. I'd rather describe how caddies categorized their totes.

Already I mentioned the big tippers, the tightwads, and the grouches. These three need no explanation. However, we classified those who fit different descriptions as:

NERVOUS NELLIES: Took too many frustrations out on caddies. We couldn't be quiet or still enough. Generally thinks a caddie should be standing some place else even when he couldn't hear or see them. Won't even putt if an automobile or motorcycle is traveling near by.

SLOW POKES: He holds up the whole golf course. They learn to waste time. Never know when it's his turn to shoot. Always fiddling around lighting a cigarette or reaching in the ball pocket for a ball or tee when he has the honor.

THE ANGRY PALS OF THE DEVIL: Caddies learn to keep an eye on him and get far enough away as he makes a pass at a golf ball. Caddies want room to duck a flying mashie. We had one member (a lawyer, mind you) once he teed his ball up on Number 1, cursed it the whole 18 holes. He used such language only the devil's advocate could have taught him. I might add and perhaps it's no surprise to you, this guy died at the age of about 50 of a heart attack.

THE CRANKS: Also take too many frustrations out on caddies. Probably scared of their wives or bosses. Their caddies catch hell when he's holding the flagstick properly. This guy wants the caddie holding it on the other side of the hole. If the wind is rattling the cloth flag, the caddie hears about it. Grumbles about most everything.

THE BRAGGERS: Got the best car, clothes, best job, best wife, best kids. The best set of golf clubs. In reality he has the heaviest bag as he carries the best of rainwear, golf balls, etc. and the poorest golf score.

THE SKINFLINTS: He makes a big deal out of giving you a dime tip. He acts like a caddie ought to be grateful as he's probably sacrificing a fine cigar.

THE PACK HORSES: Comes out of the locker room with a sweater, towel, quart of scotch, sun glasses, a dozen balls, and expects us to tote this stuff for 18 holes. His bag is usually the size of a rain barrel.

THE CHEATERS: These guys who think every body is dumb. Fudges on marking his ball. And has bad arithmetic. Takes 5 to get on the green and 3 putts and tells the caddie keeping score he had a 6.

Yes, when it comes to education, caddies learn a lot from the various totes. Caddies get "people smarts". Since I caddied for doctors, lawyers, bankers, merchants, politicians, accountants, etc., I saw and served them when their hair was down. A man displays his patience, self discipline, fellowship, generosity, arithmetic, humility, anger and some other good and bad qualities.

Since I've played golf for many years after leaving the caddie ranks and have played and competed with many many golfers, I'll have to say I can tell more about a person playing 18 holes with him than sharing a class in psychology.

I'm getting away from caddie stories but later I'll give you a description of what I think golf really is.

CADDIE LANGUAGE

Caddies not only had nicknames for other caddies, golf pros, maintenance workers, and clubhouse personnel. But, they had names for various parts of the golf course, golf clubs, type of golf shots, and descriptions of various circumstances.

Some of their definitions are carried over to golfers of today. Some of the language Rock caddies used was original and yet some was tradition and a carry over from the early Scots.

Here is how a Rock Spring caddie dictionary might read had one been printed:

PUT ON   term used when caddie master assigns a caddie to a golf bag

GYPPED   term caddies used when a caddie's name was called for a tote and he wasn't present

KICKED OFF   term used to describe caddie being fired or laid off for a week or more

RIGS   term shouted by another caddie when caddie buys a candy bar or sodie (soda pop) meaning buyer must save last bite or swig for another caddie

LINE UP — the time caddie master arrives for work (7 a.m.) and lines up caddies as to the order of their arrival and puts their names (or nicknames) on the LINE UP sheet

DANCE
FLOOR — putting green

FROG HAIR — collar around the putting green

SAND TRAP — sand bunker; also referred to as "on the beach" and "nutmeg parlor"

PIN — flagstick

CUP — hole on the putting green

PILL — golf ball

O.B. — ball hit out of bounds

SNUCKLE
BERRIES — portion of golf course of tall weeds, vines, briars, etc. making most golf balls hit there unplayable

SNUCKLED — player's ball behind a tree or in a tough lie

TEE BOX	wooden structure at each teeing ground containing white sand and a bucket of water for building a sand mound for a tee and for cleaning golf balls
BIG BALL WASHER	pond, lake, or body of water. When player's ball landed in a lake caddies said, "It landed in the BIG BALL WASHER."
PUSHER	putter
BIG HAMMER	driver
DOUBLES	caddie carrying two bags (an assignment when they ran out of caddies)
WORM BURNER	player's drive that skids along the ground
FROZEN ROPE	low line drive
SNAP FADE	better known as a SHANK; ball hit on the hosel of an iron shot
SLICE	ball curving to the right for a right handed player; left handers, just the opposite

BANANA
BALL   big slice

DUCK
HOOK   a low flying drive that curves sharply to
              the left for a right handed player; just
              the opposite for left handers

FORE GOD   term caddies used to describe a skied
              tee shot

THROW-UP
ZONE   important short missable putt

SNOWMAN   score of 8 on a hole

GIMME   ball laying real close to the hole

ON THE
LEATHER   term used for GIMME'S; early on,
              grips for golf clubs were spiraled on
              shafts for approximately 16 inches. The
              leather grip was used as a gauge to
              determine GIMME'S. If the ball was
              within the 16 inches, he was not
              required to finish. In other words, he
              had no chance of missing the putt. It
              saved wear and tear around the hole.

FANNED
THE BALL   player took a swing and did not move
                  the golf ball

GALLAGHER'S
ISLAND   a thin, flat portion of the No. 1 hole
                  across the creek about 175 yards right
                  where a dentist member, Dr.
                  Gallagher's drive landed about 7 out of
                  10 times

SPINACH   another name for the "rough"

IN JAIL   the woods

19th HOLE   clubhouse bar

CHILI
DIPPER   to hit turf behind the ball

ZEPPELIN   a skied shot; not as high as a "FORE
                  GOD"

BALL
JACKER   player who twists the grass or heels the
                  turf to improve his lie

DEW
SWEEPERS   first foursome off the tee in the early
                  morning

CAT BOX	another name for sand trap
FRIED EGG	buried lie in the sand
YIP THE PUTT	uncontrollable body spasm on a short, important putt
AMPUTATE THE DOG LEG	cut the corner while playing a dog leg hole
WIND CHEATER	low flying drive
HAND MASHIE	otherwise known as a "shoulder wedge"; an illegitimate shot whereby the ball is thrown from a poor lie to a better spot when others aren't looking

MY FIRST REAL GOLF CLUB

As a 10 year old, I made a trade to an older neighborhood caddie, Del Naville, 13 used balls for a hickory shafted jigger. Jigger is a name given to a club used primarily for chipping. It had the loft of a mashie (No. 5 iron) and the blade was thinner than a standard mashie head. It's shaft is a little shorter than a standard mashie shaft.

I worshipped this golf club. My first round of golf as an 11 year old caddie, I shot Rock Springs in 56. Using only one club - the jigger. Yes, I putted with it too. That club we used for golf in Smith's pasture and I carried it back and forth to the caddie yard. I'd ditch this club near the barn on occasion when I was afraid bully caddies would break it.

Since I lived in middle town and several of my caddie friends lived in the neighborhood, many are the times we played golf all the way home from the caddie yard. We were little gamblers, playing for pennies and nickels. These games were like this. It was really more like golf croquet, as we played from one telephone pole to another to a manhole cover to the left rear tire of the Model T parked up the street to the big elm tree on the corner and so on. We lost some balls in the street drainage sewers.

I had a six hole miniature golf course in my yard that I often played using this club. It took about three years before this club got away from me. If I had it today, it would be worth about $100. Later my older sister, Flossie bought me three golf clubs at an auction sale. One was a Fancy Face Spoon (No. 3 wood). Collectors would pay several hundred dollars today for that golf club.

The older caddie friend, Bernard (Baldy) Wright who took me to the caddie yard in 1928 when I caddied for the first time, had a Fancy Face Driver that we used for driving contests on Number 1 tee before LINE UP. He's the kid who early on could hit a golf ball about 100 yards with a wooden walking cane.

When "Baldy" showed with this driver before LINE UP, all the caddies interested in hitting drives went to Number 1 tee and played "Shortest Drive Retrieves all the Balls". Usually six to eight caddies took part. I probably was the smallest caddie in these contests. Of course, I ran out and retrieved the balls many times. When the balls were rounded up, we did it again and again 'till the caddie master showed for LINE UP. Later, I learned how to hit some big drives and seldom had to do the retrieving.

We used this driver so much, we beat the Fancy Face insert out of the driver face.

Before LINE UP, we caddies also had putting contest on the practice green. This was a no-no as we left evidence in the morning dew. We learned not to engage in 5 cent putting skins when dew covered the putting green.

In our caddie days, one maintenance worker wiped the early morning dew off the greens with a long bamboo fishing pole. Some golf courses still use this method today. Others do it by dragging a garden hose across the green in a circular manner. Some times the dew is removed from fairways by two workers in golf carts dragging a long garden hose. One cart on the left side of the fairway, one on the right side. The cart drivers stay even with each other as they drag the hose between them covering the full width of the fairway.

THE CADDIE STRIKE

In the summer of 1936, the caddies decided 30 cents for a nine hole tote wasn't enough money. So at noon on a Saturday, all of us refused to caddie unless caddie fees were raised to 40 cents for nine holes, 75 cents for 18 holes. A-class and B-class caddies both to get this same pay. Since over 35 members were without caddies it created quite a disturbance for awhile. Lou Miller was pro and pleaded with us to tote this day; and he would talk to the proper caddie committee and report back to us in a few days.

Since there were several foursomes ready to tee off on Number 1 tee with no golf clubs or caddies, some of these members took it on themselves to okay the demands if we'd break up the strike and tote today.

So all of us immediately said okay and grabbed a golf bag and hustled up to Number 1 tee. The next day, Lou Miller announced the new caddie fees were as we demanded: 40 cents for 9 holes and 75 cents for 18.

The strike lasted about an hour.

CADDIES AS PIN SETTERS

Later in the fall of this same year, 1936, Acme Bowling Alley opened eight more lanes. Several of us caddies got jobs as pin setters. I'm 16 years old now and this pin setting job was mostly for 7 p.m. and 9 p.m. bowling leagues on week days. Saturday and Sundays we set pins for open play from noon until 11 p.m.

Our pay was 4 cents per game. In league play, two five man teams use two alleys and roll three games. That's a total of 30 games on 2 alleys engaging two pin boys. Each gets credit for 15 games. That's 15 x 4 cents = 60 cents per league. It takes two hours for leagues to finish and bowling alleys schedule two leagues per evening at 7 and 9 p.m. We usually set two leagues every evening. Pay: $1.20 and we all had social security numbers and it was deducted from our pay. We were paid each night when bowling was over at about 11:30 p.m.

I elected to tell you this bowling job for the following story. Most of us pin boys lived in middle town Alton and about two miles from the bowling alley. Most times we hoofed it home.

One of our pin setter caddie friends, Lucien Curry had an old jalopy Dodge and often we gave him a dime for gas to drive us home.

Once he parked across the street form the bowling alley and six pin boys piled in the car with Lucien and he wouldn't start the motor 'till he had 60 cents (a dime from each of us). Now, Lucien got the transmission stuck in reverse. The car would only move in reverse. Lucien elected to back that old car all the way from downtown Alton to middle town. Since it's near midnight and not much traffic, he made it while hanging his head out the window to see where he was backing. The most hilarious ride I've even had. Lucien wasn't too good a driver and took up the whole street in several blocks. The caddies were laughing and heckling Lucien and he was cussin' and hollering for us to shut up.

LOU MILLER AND 640 CASES OF COKE

You've met the golf pro, Lou Miller. I'd mentioned he had the reputation of being close with a buck. He was a hard guy to win a bet from. One of the best competitors I've known. He often challenged members and caddies to a putting game for a COKE. For these stakes, he had several pigeons. Lou was an excellent putter.

One day he challenged my caddie friend "Hub" Turley. As Hub and I were sitting watching Lou do some practice putting, Lou said, "C'mon, Hub, I'll putt you for a COKE." Lou didn't know how good Hub really was and didn't know Hub and I both knew every break in the slants of this putting green as we putted by moonlight many many times.

Of all the golf I've watched, this putting contest was the best. Hub quickly knocked in a putt. Then another and another and had Lou six COKES hooked before Lou knew what was happening. Lou, who hates to lose, said, "Hub, let's putt for 5 COKES." Hub still is holing everything. Hub had Lou hooked for so many COKES, they started betting cases of COKES. At one point Hub had Lou down 640 cases of COKE as they were doubling and doubling. As they putted for 640 cases of COKE, Lou knocked in a no brainer and they ended up all even. Lou did have the courtesy to buy Hub a COKE.

That was the last time Lou challenged Hub on the putting green. What I would have given to see Hub on being 640 cases of COKE up, walk off the putting green telling "Uncle Louie", "That's enough COKE to last me a life time, I quit."

We caddies had many such putting contests for pennies and nickels.

During my caddie days, the Pace family lived next to Number 2 green on Salu Road. The two oldest boys, Robert (Bones) Pace and Jesse (Judge) Pace were caddies. Several of their younger brothers also caddied later.

In the fall and winter months several of us caddies congregated at this Pace residence. Sometimes no golfers were on the course and we played Numbers 3, 4, and 5 over and over. These holes are on the north side of Salu Road while the other six holes are on the south side. These three holes are farthest from the clubhouse and maintenance shed. We kept a lookout for Cliff, the maintenance supervisor, as he periodically checked on us. We just ditched in the woods and out of sight until he was gone. Golf resumed when all was clear.

We also had putting games on Number 2 green. As I said, the Pace boys lived but 40 yards from this green. Number 2 green was along the south side of Salu road and Pace's lived on the north side. Number 2 green was tucked under a hill and out of view from the clubhouse and maintenance shed. We posted a lookout at the crest of this hill whereas a caddie laid on his belly and kept an eye out for Cliff. He knew what we were doing and occasionally came barreling over Number 8 and

Number 6 fairways in a Model A pickup truck trying to catch us on the green.

When the lookout signaled "Cliff is coming", we got out on Salu Road before Cliff arrived at the scene. He knew we'd been on the green but couldn't do a thing about it. Sometimes, Mr. Pace was standing in the yard overlooking this situation. Cliff wasn't about to challenge Mr. Pace's sweet little boys.

We all played golf every Monday except when it was raining or had been, making the course too soft. No rain checks, as that was it for that week. Several times four to eight of us caddies hoofed it over to Muny when we didn't get to play Monday golf at Rock. A phone call to Muny to see if it was open for play. Green fees at Muny were 25 cents for 9 holes.

Muny was about one mile from Rock caddie yard and we caddies would cut through Oakwood cemetery and start teeing it up on Number 2 tee. Then play 2, 3, 4, 5, 6, 7, 8, 9. Sometimes we didn't have to pay for those eight holes. But when they charged us caddies 25 cents, we said, "We started on Number 2 so we get to play Number 1. That, they'd let us do. When we finished Number 1, we didn't quit. We continued to play Numbers 2, 3, 4, 5, and 6. Since Number 6 green was close to Number 2 tee and close to our path back through the cemetery, we then left the golf course. So we managed to play 14 holes for 25 cents. Actually they didn't care but let us believe we were pulling the wool over their eyes. They knew we were Rock caddies and interested in golf.

On one of these trips over to Muny on a rather rainy day (no golf this Monday at Rock), I was wearing a white golf cap. As mentioned, the 19 cent cap from Snyders. Mom washed these caps as they got dirty. This distorted the bill of the cap and they got to looking bad. One day I got a bright idea. My sisters had white shoe polish and I used it to renew my white cap. It looked real neat. As we walked in the rain to Muny, the cap was getting wetter and wetter. The white shoe polish started running down my face. I looked like one of Frankenstein's family members. These caddie friends got to laughing and tacked the nickname "Shoe Polish" on me. This nickname lasted a couple of months.

Other nicknames I've had caddies plant on me were "Second Hand Man", "Satch", "Eck", "Bald Eagle", "Eagle", "Eagle Eye", and "Chris".

BARNEY'S TOTE

One day in 1938, veteran caddie, Barney Fahrig got the tote for Hale Jones (World's Best Trap Shooter). Hale who was associated with Western Cartridge Company, traveled around the world with his guns setting all kinds of records breaking clay pigeons.

Hale handed Barney a dozen Wilson K-28 golf balls (Wilson's best ball in those days) on Number 1 tee. I was one of the caddies in this foursome. Hale teed up a brand new K-28 and hit it right into deep woods. A huge banana ball. He followed this drive with four more huge banana balls. That's five balls sliced so deep in the woods that he wouldn't let us caddies go hunt for 'em. His sixth tee shot landed in the creek that cuts diagonally across the fairway. It's lost. At the creek Hale slices three approach shots to the green out of bounds right in deep alfalfa. All three were lost. That's nine lost balls.

He finishes out the hole and the foursome goes to Number 2 tee. Hale proceeds to slice three balls out of bounds. That's the twelve K-28s. But Hale's not counting and asks Barney for another ball. Barney says, "There ain't no more". And Hale replies, "You mean you lost that whole dozen?" Barney says, "You're the guy that knocked them off the golf course." With that, Hale says to Barney, "You're fired." Barney dropped the golf bag from his shoulder and headed back to the caddie yard. To Hale, Barney says, "If I couldn't play golf any better than you, I'd quit." By this time the players and caddies are laughing. Hale turns to his fellow competitors and announces, "I might not be able to hit a golf ball, but I can shoot a shotgun".

This story is true and never ever have I heard of a golfer losing a dozen balls and not off the second tee yet.

Some food for thought. Four of us caddies went golf ball hunting as soon as we finished. We found 11 of them.

RED RYAN

Red Ryan was the oldest caddie at Rock in the late 1930s. He was 24 years old and had no home. He slept in the furnace room many nights. He sometimes caddied barefoot. He mastered the art of stepping on a ball lodging it between his big toe and next toe. With this maneuver, he was able to carry his player's ball to a better position without players knowing as he was neither bending down or kicking. It got him some illegitimate tips.

CADDIES TAKING A RIDE IN A NEW CADILLAC CONVERTIBLE

Rock Spring C.C. had a member who headed up the Cadillac Automobile Agency. His wife drove a pretty blue Cadillac Convertible. She liked to park her automobile next to the steps that led to the ladies' locker room. This parking spot, kept the driver delivering coal to the coal bin from backing up to the coal shute.

One day, her car had to be moved. She was down on Number 1 green when a caddie ran down to her to tell her she had to move her car. Her car keys were in the golf bag. The caddie told her if she gave him the keys, he'd move it for her. She said "okay, and leave the keys with the caddie master."

The caddie moved the car alright. He took three boys with him and left the parking lot and traveled through Upper Alton for nearly an hour. These caddies went by two of their girlfriends' houses, honked the horn and had a ball. They didn't get caught. What a sight: four caddies in a brand new Cadillac convertible. A ride fit for a king.

Another time, caddies caught the caddie master napping and went for a ride in a member's Hubmobile. The keys were in the ignition and four caddies pushed this car and got it rolling down and out of the driveway without starting the motor until they were out of sight. Returned it after about an hour joy ride.

Unusual Totes

There was one foursome at Rock who took five caddies three or four times a year. These were times they were celebrating something. Each took a caddie and the fifth caddie's assignment was to carry a gallon pickle jar. The jar was once used for pickles, but today it's full of gin rickies and ice. The caddie carrying this pickle jar was furnished a bath towel (to wrap around the jar) and an umbrella to keep the sun off it.

This was a day when the tips were very generous.

Once while caddying in this foursome, these guys got through nine holes, hit drives (or rather hacked their drives) on Number 1 of the second nine and decided to quit. We caddies retrieved the balls and got paid for 18 holes plus tips.

After leaving the caddie ranks, my younger caddie friend, Paul (Bite the Dust) Owens told me of a couple of times he and Dal Ray (Dog Patch) Pace were hired as the fifth and sixth caddie for a foursome of party guys. Their job was to carry a bushel basket that contained bottle beer, bourbon, and soda.

MR. GRAVES AND GOLF BALL TESTING

As mentioned, Mr. Graves was the pro at Rock Spring C.C. in the 1920s and early 1930s. The late 1920s and 1930s were my caddie years.

In these days, golf balls were all three piece balls. Most golf balls first started from a frozen ball about the same diameter as a quarter (25 cent piece) that was made of rubber (some solid and some liquid filled). Then this small ball was wrapped with thin rubber windings. These windings wrapped the ball to a diameter to accommodate a rather soft balata cover. This cover was from about 1/16" to 3/16" thick. With all the manufacturers' efforts with this process, balls were not as uniform as they are today. (However, today over 99% of all golf balls are out of balance a little bit. I'll give you proof later.)

Mr. Graves took steps to give balls he played with a few tests. First he shoved them through a ring gauge several times, rotating them each time he passed them through the gauge. Balls that proved to be slightly egg shaped, Mr. Graves discarded. Then he snapped them down to the concrete floor and their "click" meant something. His ears were in tune as balls had to sound right. Then, while standing, he tested their rebound qualities by holding one in each hand from forehead height and dropping them to the concrete floor. Some that rebounded poorly were discarded.

From 10 to 12 balls, he now has about a half dozen that he's satisfied are worthy of his play.

Now, (the very first time I witnessed the above) he's ready for the final test of these balls. Says to me, "Mike, hand me that container" and points to a coffee mug size metal container on the back of the shop work bench. I reached for it. At first I thought it was nailed down. I looked at him. He's laughing and says, "Go ahead. Pick it up." That little container weighed five pounds or more. Mr. Graves says, "What's in that container?" I didn't know. Then he rotated it and a small label read, "mercury". Since mercury is an extremely heavy element, Mr. Graves got several caddies (and members) to hand him it. His little joke.

Now Mr. Graves takes the lid off this container and puts a golf ball in the mercury. The ball sits up like a ship at sea. A golf ball will not sink in this mercury. Now the golf ball is sitting up and Mr. Graves puts his index finger on the golf ball and his thumb on the rim of the container and gives the ball a flick to make it rotate as fast as he can. He repositions each ball several times and makes them rotate. From how these balls rotate, he determines their balance characteristics. If they spun quite freely, they displayed good balance. If they sort of hopped as they spun, this suggested to Mr. Graves that they were out of balance. He played only with those that spun freely.

Now, I'll give you a method that apparently Mr. Graves didn't know, for you to test your own golf balls. Had Mr. Graves known this method you are about to learn, I'm sure he would have used it.

Let me repeat, "99% of all golf balls today are slightly out of balance or slightly egg shaped or both. Most golfers won't pay any attention to me on this statement. And 90% of golfers need not bother with this test.

Since my years on the golf course are old enough to qualify for social security, here are some comments I've heard on the putting green. No doubt you too have heard most of 'em.

"Did you see that ball break uphill?" "Did you see that ball get up to the lip of the cup and rock back?" "Did you see that ball stop and then move slightly right (or left)?" "Oh, that ball can't break that much on that short putt." "What made that ball hop like a rabbit for the first ten feet of a long putt?" "That ball rolled in a path like the letter J."

Then you've seen putts going straight at the hole but are speeding and you just know the hole won't stop it, but it gets to the hole and sort of dives in it when you believe this putt should have left a six to ten footer coming back.

Some balls drop in the hole, disappear for a moment and rim out. And how many times have you been reaching in the hole for a ball you felt sure would be in the bottom of the cup and as it rolled up to the cup suddenly flopped left or right and hung on the lip?

My golfing friends, these are not all optical illusions. In most cases these conditions are caused by rolling slightly egg shaped balls or out of balance balls or both.

Here's the test. You'll only need water, epsom salts, dish washing liquid, and a small jar. A one pound peanut butter jar is ideal. However, most any size is okay. But don't get a jar smaller than the peanut butter jar. Fill your jar about half full with water. Drop a golf ball in it. It will sink to the bottom. Now add epsom salt. Stir it until it dissolves. Keep adding epsom salts until the ball floats. Then add three or four drops of dish washing liquid.

Now you have a Magic Ball Balancing Solution. At least let's call it that. Actually this solution is finding for you the heavy portion of the ball.

Here's what's happening. As the ball floats in this solution, gravity is pulling the heavy side down. The dish washing liquid is making the ball slick so as to allow it to rotate freely releasing the surface tension. (Some epsom salts have an ingredient that makes it slick going down your throat and makes using dish washing liquid unnecessary.)

As the golf ball floats in this solution, a spot on the ball (about the size of a 25 cent coin) is above the water level. Now take a marking pen and put a dot in the center of this spot. Now you can spin this ball forever and this dot will come back to the same location. If it were to be a perfectly balanced ball, that dot would appear anywhere. (In spinning several hundred balls, only twice, did I run on to a perfectly balanced one.)

Some balls are so far off balance that as you spin them in this magic solution they act as if they want to jump out of the jar.

Since this mark is 180 degrees from the heavy portion, your ball now has a message for you. If this ball could talk it'd say, "When putting, position me with the dot straight up. This assures you the heavy portion of me is resting on the green. As you strike me, the heavy spot will travel in my rotating line to the hole."

Get it? Should this heavy side be right or left it will cause the ball to veer off line. As you stroke a putt, you send it toward the hold with forward thrust. This action overcomes weight until it slows down nearing the hole. As the ball is now moving very slowly, the weight is the influencing factor as to whether the ball continues to roll straight or veer off line.

When I said, "90% of golfers need not be concerned with this test." Today most of you play two piece balls. This construction eliminates the winding process and the balls are more uniform for roundness and balance. Those of you who think you have an accurate putting stroke will do yourself a favor using this test.

The Magic Ball Balancing Solution is a great conversation piece for golf groups or parties, etc. You'll have fun demonstrating your knowledge.

There are gadgets on the market to do this same thing. Most of them spin the ball and centrifugal force positions the heavy side of the ball to the bottom of this gadget. These gadgets usually require batteries and are expensive. Why buy one when epsom salts costs but pennies?

You might be surprised to know most touring pros play with balls that are 99% of perfect balance. Many of these golf pros who make their living with golf clubs and balls carry a ring gauge and periodically check the balls they are playing. They often knock 'em out of round. Big swingers like John Daly knock them out of round quite often.

Another thing the pros do is change balls after each hole. And not putting it back in play for three or four holes. Since most of the touring pros use three piece balls, it takes that long for the windings, after being flexed, to return to their original position.

Also, if you watch every move touring pros make, you'll see he (or she) reposition balls for their second and third putt. They are now taking advantage of the balance mark.

Don't waste your time using table salt, rock salt, or sea water. A golf ball will float in heavy salt water, but the liquid is so dense a ball hangs in one position no matter how much dish washing liquid you add.

As you put a mark on the ball floating in Magic Ball Balancing Solution, you'll have a little difficulty. You almost have to jab your marking pen and that pushes the ball deeper in the solution. So, let your first pass at a mark be only temporary. Carefully take the ball out of solution, wipe it very carefully. Now is the time to put a permanent mark on it. Don't make this dot any bigger than necessary. I have an extra fine permanent marking pen for this purpose and mark the ball with a very thin lined circle about 1/8" in diameter.

Another tip, don't drag out any more solution than necessary and keep a lid on the container.

Make this Magic Ball Balancing Solution any color you want by adding food coloring.

Again, I remind you, it's a great conversation piece.

CADDIE BREAKFASTS

For several years now, we Rock Spring and Muny caddies from the depression years of the 1930s and early 1940s meet every last Tuesday of the month for an 8 a.m. breakfast at D & R Diner which is a couple of miles east of Alton. We rehash stories of our caddie days. All of us are retired and most of us did a hitch in the military in World War II. Each year we have a golf tourney at Rock Springs. All caddies who have ever toted for fee are welcome for the breakfasts and golf tourney. About 30 caddies take part in the golf tournament which is a four man scramble. We make reservations after the tournament for dinner, have some sudsy refreshments and award prizes.

At these, there are plenty of laughs at caddie stories they tell. One caddie tells of the time he lost a ball for his player on a four foot putt. It was a down hiller that rolled off the green and into a ground hog hole.

Another caddie tells of a tote for an out of town lady guest of a lady member. Just the two of them played. On No. 1 green, the guest had about a 20 foot putt from a spot on the green west of the hole. In those days, the out of bounds fence (three strand barbed wire) was about 15 feet from the frog hair on the east side of the green. Her caddie was holding the flagstick and she whacked her putt so hard it went out of bounds. The two caddies could hardly contain themselves. She looked over to her lady host and said, "fast grass". The four of them broke out laughing.

Another story one caddie told was about a time he caddied for Spencer T. Olin. A day he lugged Mr. Olin's clubs for 36 holes. The day Mr. Olin won the Alton City Tournament. Caddie fees were 75 cents for 18 holes. So Mr. Olin owed this caddie $1.50. Mr. Olin gave him a twenty dollar bill. The first one he'd ever seen. Took this bill home and showed it to his mother. She said, "Where'd you steal it?"

Still another Muny caddie told a story of a tote he had. Muny caddie fees at this time (mid 1930s) were 25 cents for 9 holes. This guy gave his caddie 30 cents. Then after a minute or so he said to the caddie, "Give me that nickel back. It'll buy a good cigar."

These caddies like to bring up this story on me. This story happened in the summer of 1940 and I'm 20 years old. I left the caddie ranks the previous year. Rock Spring C.C. held a golf tournament called "Rock Spring Invitational". You had to be invited to be a contestant. I was one of 16 local golfers who got an invite. All the St. Louis district hot shots were invited. It was an 18 hole Sunday afternoon affair with about 36 contestants.

Since Rock Spring is a 9 hole golf course, they had sets of two tees on every hole. We played the short tees on the first nine, back tees on the back nine. Par for the golf course was 36. On the front nine, I shot a 40 and thought I'd blown myself out. Then I arrived at the sixth hole on the back nine having made two birdies. So I'm two under par for the previous five holes. A caddie friend informed me that 36 was the best score posted for the front nine. Now the wheels in my 20 year old brain get to clicking. It tells me, "If these hot shots from St. Louis can't shoot the short nine in better than 36, they won't shoot better from the back tees on the finishing nine."

So I reason a score of even par 72 just might win the tourney. And all I need is two more birdies for a four under par 32 to go with that 40. I now tee it up and with about 25 people in the gallery watching me, I'm going to crush a drive. Guess who got "crushed"? Me. I fanned that sucker. These caddies are still laughing at me. (or is it - they are laughing WITH me.)

The 32 of my dreams turned out to be 37. My 77 was a sixth place tie with Spencer T. Olin. The best score of the Alton contestants. A score of 70 won the event.

GOLF

Golf is the most humbling field of endeavor we can participate in. Golf has it's bitter disappointments as well as it's rewarding moments. Like life, huh! I've told you the story of my fanning a tee shot while challenging to win a tournament with about 25 people watching. I was 20 years old at the time. At that time, I felt like jumping in the nearest garbage can and disappearing.

Another disappointing round of golf happened this way. A golfer likes to shoot his age as early as possible. Sam Snead shot 62 when he was 62. At the age of 68, I missed a 28 inch putt on the last hole to rob me of a 68 at Rock. The putt went in the hole and rimmed out. The 69 that I actually shot was the lowest score I'd shot in almost 50 years. Yet, I went away from the golf course disappointed. When I should have been ever so grateful to have shot 69. That's golf.

Golf is a game most every one can play. Age has very little to do with who may play. I've played golf as early as six year old and as I write this book, I'm 76 years old and still playing golf. I tell my friends, I'm going to play till I'm 100 and then re-evaluate the situation.

Physically handicapped people play golf. I play with a fellow caddie who has but one arm. Many play who have much more major medical and physical problems. Dennis Walters is paralyzed from the waist down. No control over his legs, he heads up golf shows around the United States giving exhibits while hitting balls from a sitting position in a specially built golf car. It's absolutely amazing what this man can do.

Golf has been a big part of my life. This caddie story is only a part of it. Early in my youth, I saw golf as a recreation and an opportunity to earn a few nickels. As I continued to play it, it gradually took on a more fruitful meaning. Most sports imitate war. Golf imitates life.

What better education might I have had then spending all my teenage years in the caddie yard and on the golf course. It taught me how to get along with a whole bunch of kids in my age group. It taught me how to deal with grown ups, other than my parents, who were employing me to pack their golf clubs and provide a worthy service. Though I didn't know it then, caddying exposed me to the real world and allowed me the privilege to grow. I'm ever so grateful.

While caddying for members of Rock Spring C.C., they were not only teaching me how to get the golf ball in the hole but more important how one must or must not deal with emotions. They taught me lessons on patience, anxieties, anger, hostilities, and discipline.

They taught me how necessary it is to play the game fair and square, to have compassion for my fellow competitors, and to be courteous at all times. I now understand courtesy is the language of love.

I love the challenges golf presents. Every golf shot challenges you. And no matter how good your execution of the shot, it can be improved on until you knock it in the hole.

You continue to be challenged on a golf course no matter what your level of play. The three and a half footer for your first birdie, your short putt to break a 100 for the first time. Your first round to shoot par or your first time to break 50. Your first tournament win, etc. These are all challenges and I can remember most of them as I grew in my world of golf. I've quit commenting to people who say, "I can't see what you see in hitting the ball, go chase it and hit it again." I'm hoping they stay off the golf course.

It's been said over and over that "variety is the spice of life". Golf gives us variety like no other sport. No 18 hole golf course is laid out the same as another. As a matter of fact, no two holes are exactly the same. And even the same hole on different playing days changes characteristics due to the hole being cut in a different location of the green. And green speed differs due to moisture and the last time it was mowed. Wind, temperature and moisture have a way of altering shot distance and ball trajectory.

Most other sports, like football, baseball, tennis, soccer are played within chalked lines and foul poles. These sports are played on repetitious, boring box-like grounds by the young engaged in war-like games. No place for a 76 year old like me and most of these war like sports have no place for a person reaching their mid-30s.

Golf can be played by most everyone. Golf doesn't care who you are. Male or female. Young or old, or what color your skin or your religious beliefs. It doesn't care if you play barefoot. However, I'm in favor of some kind of dress code. In my early caddie days, women wore long skirts and big brim hats. Men wore plus fours (knickers), long sleeve shirts (mostly white) with neckties.

Not until the 1940s did the touring pro's change from long sleeve shirts and neckties to the more comfortable short sleeved shirt and slacks. I have a whole bunch of pictures from the 1920s and 1930s of my idols (Bobby Jones, Walter Hagen, Gene Sarazen) playing in long sleeve white shirts and neckties.

Bobby Locke, one of the British golfing greats and labeled the best putter of all time, while playing in the 1947 U.S.Open in St. Louis wore plus fours, a long sleeve white shirt, and necktie. I was in the gallery on the final 18. Locke was paired with Ben Hogan. Ben was also one of my favorites and I followed this twosome for many holes.

Most golf courses of today are manicured to perfection. It's a pleasure to just walk the links. You're out with nature at it's best. Lakes, trees, shrubs, creeks, flowers, sunshine, breeze, clouds, sun, etc. You get a feeling of walking with your Creator in this beautiful creation with birds singing and chirping. And occasionally, a deer, fox, rabbit, squirrel appears along the way. Canadian honkers are attracted to the lakes and turf on golf courses. Once a couple of years ago I counted 225 Canadian Geese in the fairway I was playing in Kalamazoo, Michigan. Yes, I marvel at sites and scenes on and around golf courses.

As I've said, playing golf, you always have competition. Even when playing alone. Trying to beat the best score you have ever shot is a rewarding chase. The devil's advocate who sits in the fragile area of the golfing brain will try it's best to trip you up. You'll have plenty of opportunity to evaluate your probabilities for success while the devil's advocate encourages you to defeat yourself.

PLAYING COMPETITIVE GOLF

By that, I mean entering a golf tournament and competing for a prize. The most rewarding thing, should you win a golf tournament, is not the trophy but your victory over yourself. For a golf professional to win on the pro tour, he (or she) must have skills in both shot execution and golf course management. Swinging a golf club is only a part of it. As the great Bobby Jones once said, "Competitive golf is played on a five and a half inch long course: the distance between the ears."

Bobby Jones won the Grand Slam of golf. That is, he won all four (The U.S. Open, U.S. Amateur, British Open and British Amateur) in the same year. With no more worlds to conquer, he retired from competitive golf at the age of 28 in 1930. He continued to play but these later playing days were cut short by a crippling muscular disease. His inability to play the game he had once found so fulfilling seemed to deepen his appreciation and understanding of it. Jones observed that golf "is usually played with the outward appearance of great dignity. It is, nevertheless, a game of considerable passion, either of the explosive type, or that which burns inwardly and scars the soul."

Jeff Sluman, touring professional golfer, who has done well on the tour, has experienced the highest of the highs and the lowest of the lows, offers the most elo-

119

quent description of life as a professional golfer. "I hate this game," he says, "and I can't wait till tomorrow to play it again."

What Jones and Sluman said rings a bell with most competitive golfers.

Yes, these two guys are only a couple of many who have experienced nervous frustration in the heat of the competitions. They've had the task of club selection, judging ball trajectory, slants and speed of the greens, etc. while the nerves are jumping. The obstacles on the golf course aren't as hard to master as the lumps in their throat, butterflies in their bellies, or goose pimples on the heart.

Yes, and you get no where on your fat pocket book, good looks, family influence. No team mate for help. You are alone with your emotions for club selection and shot execution while the devil's advocate tries to trip you up.

Bobby Jones said it so eloquently, "it burns inwardly and scars the soul". Not too many contestants can stand the pressure. It takes real guts and then some. There's a long list of players who have come real close to winning the Open. They just didn't have a shot they needed on the final hole. It's been said, "you just don't win the Open, the other players just throw it away."

Go ahead. Play the game. Above anything else, have fun and learn to laugh at yourself. I'll have to tell you this story. My daughter Martie, who is 35 years old, lives in Kalamazoo, Michigan. She has played a big part in the manuscript for this book. I write it in long hand, send it to her and she types it on her computer and corrects my spelling, and organizes my thoughts and writings.

She and I were playing Milham Park Golf Course near her home in Kalamazoo a few years ago and she hit a dumb looking shot and I started laughing. She says, "Why are you laughing at me, Dad?" I said, "Martie, I'm not laughing at you, I'm laughing WITH you." She said, "Then how come I'm not laughing?" I said, "Martie, it's just a game. Relax and enjoy it." She did just that and had some fine shots on the remaining holes.

One final word to beginners. If you've never played a round of golf, you'll only need two clubs for the first 6 or 8 rounds. These two clubs are a "mashie" (No. 5 iron) and putter. Play every shot with the mashie until you are near enough to the hole to just roll the ball. Then use your putter. When you have made swings at the ball to double the par, pick up your ball and put it in your pocket. On par 3 holes, you can't make more than 6. On par 4's, 8 is your biggest score and 10 is your max on par 5's. This advice is when playing with more experienced players. You are expected to play slow, but please don't over do it. With nothing but shots hit with the mashie, you'll find out how versatile this club really is, which will be valuable information as you progress in golf.

You'll have a chance to develop a decent golf swing and gain some confidence. The driver is the hardest club to use. If you have one, lock it up in a closet until you've played at least 25 rounds.

Having caddied for a whole bunch of golfers with full sets of clubs, that would be my advice to a large percentage of them. Oh so many didn't know how to use any of their clubs. If I were to go to the golf course today with only these two clubs, the score I'd shoot would be very close to the score using all 14 clubs. So would most golfers.

In the beginning of this book, you learned some golf etiquette. You'll keep learning. Don't be afraid to ask questions. There are no dumb questions. But you will get some dumb answers. As beginners, most everybody wants to help you. Most of them will only confuse you. Get your advice from the pro. The time to take lessons is only after playing 6 or 8 times using your own smarts. You'll have a better understanding if you've played and experienced the dumb swings you've taken.

If you have kids that are ready to play, let them experience a few rounds with the mashie and putter before the lessons. They too will be more receptive to professional advice. Letting kids (and adult beginners too) find out what they can do on their own is a lesson in itself. They'll more appreciate professional advice later. And playing a few times, you needn't worry that bad habits will set in. Those little scars heal easy early on.

Remember, a golf stroke is a swinging action that comes primarily from the hands. When you have good live hands, you feel the good surge of power and consequently you just let it happen. Of course the reverse of this advice is also true. When the hands are dead and ineffective you also feel the lack of power. It's then where you call upon the rest of the body to do what the hands failed to do. And that's what gets you to lunging, scooping, digging, hacking, chopping, and all that dumb stuff.

And you don't want to do that.

Play the game. Count all your strokes. Learn to laugh at yourself. Be kind to your caddies. And you'll have fun.

AFTERWARD

BY

MARTIE ECKHARD ANDERSON

DAUGHTER OF THE "GOLFMAN"

This book is only the first chapter in the life of Mike Eckhard, the Golfman. These colorful stories in the often grey days of the depression are telling. My Dad, the Golfman, has painted pictures with his life at times when there was no paint.

For you see, Mike Eckhard went on to work at Laclede Steel Company for 31 years to support six children. So where did golf fit into that picture? It did. In the crooks and crannies of his life. Honestly, I look back now with the perspective of adulthood and think, "how did Dad STILL manifest his dreams while his plate was already overflowing with responsibilities?" As the dreams of strong visionaries do, they find a way. Dad's world of golf flourished as dandelions in city sidewalks. Nothing would stop the flowering of this man and his dreams.

Here is glimpse at just a few of Mike Eckhard's golf feats.

He has always been and still is an outstanding golfer who hits the ball as straight as an arrow. As mentioned before, he won the Alton City Championship two years running. And, I watch him today compete with golfers 50 years his junior. He gives them a run for their money. He has a cool head on the golf course even though his basic temperament is excitable.

World War II took him eventually to Reims, France where, after the war, he supervised German prisoners in the rebuilding of a golf course. This course laid idle from 1939 to 1945. The clubhouse was a 16th century castle, complete with a moat surrounding it. Rumors claimed this castle was used as General Eisenhower's headquarters for a short time during the war. French, British, German, and American armies used this golf course during the war as bivouac areas. Bombs demolished two of the greens. G.I.'s dug foxholes on one of the green sites.

The French apparently thought the war wouldn't last as long as it did. The turf was removed from the greens in 1939, rolled in neat jelly roll bundles, and stacked along hedgerows near the greens. Only a few rolls were still intact in the summer of 1945. Then, this course was named OISE INTERMEDIATE SECTION GOLF COURSE. Today, it is GOLF de REIMS.

The lake which fed the moat was between Number 1 tee and green. German prisoners would dive in the lake to retrieve mishit golf balls. Remember, rubber was scarce during the war and not being used to produce golf balls!

Dad's golf career led him to start "Mike and Bud's Golf Driving Range" after returning from the war. He then taught many golf lessons for the YMCA, YWCA, for industry, and in gymnasiums throughout the area. In 1963, he opened "Mike Eckhard's Golf Shop" in our home on Highland Ave. where he sold name brand golf equipment, built and repaired thousands of golf clubs, and filled the community with the passion for playing the game.

My brother, Mike Eckhard, Jr., gave Dad this GOLF-MAN registered trademark as a father's day gift in the early '80s. He's proud of this trademark and has marketed it on thousands of items including bags, balls, clubs, towels, jewelry, shirts, hats, and jackets.

In the early 1990s, he wrote a weekly column for the "Today's Advantage" newspaper entitled "GOLF-MAN". This article contained golf tips, historical stories, jokes, and golf trivia. Favorable comments on his weekly articles from readers, many of which never played golf, persuaded Dad to write this book.

Around the Alton area, Mike Eckhard, the Golfman, has become a golf legend. His license plate reads "Golfman". And guaranteed, if you find him, he'll have yet another golf story to tell.

Do you have a story to tell??

If you have a caddie story or golf story that you would like to share, please send your story to:

Stories
Mike Eckhard
P.O. Box 33
Alton, IL 62002

Please include your full name and address with your submission. Thanks!

To order additional copies of **Sounds From the Caddie Yard,** complete the information below.

Ship to: (please print)

    Name _____

    Address _____

    City, State, Zip _____

    Day phone _____

_____ copies of *Sounds From the Caddie Yard* @

                                    $11.95 each $ _____

           Postage and handling @ $2.50 per book $ _____

        IL residents add 7% tax ($0.84 per book) $ _____

                      Total amount enclosed $ _____

            Make checks payable to *Mike Eckhard*

        Send to: **GOLFMAN, Mike Eckhard**
               P.O. Box 33 • Alton, IL 62002

To order additional copies of **Sounds From the Caddie Yard,** complete the information below.

Ship to: (please print)

    Name _____

    Address _____

    City, State, Zip _____

    Day phone _____

_____ copies of *Sounds From the Caddie Yard* @

                                    $11.95 each $ _____

           Postage and handling @ $2.50 per book $ _____

        IL residents add 7% tax ($0.84 per book) $ _____

                      Total amount enclosed $ _____

            Make checks payable to *Mike Eckhard*

        Send to: **GOLFMAN, Mike Eckhard**
               P.O. Box 33 • Alton, IL 62002